CW00972096

# Become a Total Man Magnet

Make Every Man Fall in Love with
You Instantly – Make Him Chase You Down Desperately and Beg
for Attention

## Sylvie Nicole

**Outskirts Press, Inc.**
**Denver, Colorado**

The opinions expressed in this manuscript are solely the opinions of the author and do not represent the opinions or thoughts of the publisher. The author has represented and warranted full ownership and/or legal right to publish all the materials in this book.

Become a Total Man Magnet
Make Every Man Fall in Love with You Instantly – Make Him Chase You Down Desperately and Beg for Attention
All Rights Reserved.
Copyright © 2009 Sylvie Nicole
V1.0

Cover Photo © 2009 Sylvie Nicole. All rights reserved - used with permission.

This book may not be reproduced, transmitted, or stored in whole or in part by any means, including graphic, electronic, or mechanical without the express written consent of the publisher except in the case of brief quotations embodied in critical articles and reviews.

Outskirts Press, Inc.
http://www.outskirtspress.com

ISBN: 978-1-4327-2408-5

Outskirts Press and the "OP" logo are trademarks belonging to Outskirts Press, Inc.

PRINTED IN THE UNITED STATES OF AMERICA

# Contents

# Be a Magnet for Men

There are days when nobody seems to notice you. Bad, right? Ostensibly, your hair, makeup, clothes, and everything else is as it should be—but still you get no results with men. Most likely you are not in form and have forgotten the main flirtation tips:

## No more than three

Big groups of women scare men. Three is a good number, because that way one can flirt, and the other two can make each other company. The combination of three girls is also soothing for men because of the above reason—they will not feel guilty that someone is being isolated.

## With drink in hand

You give him a wonderful occasion to start a conversation with ordering you another drink. He will not make a mistake because he can see what you already have drunk, nor will he think that you are a mercantile bitch, because you already have a drink.

## Smile

Look, forget about the overly dirty looks. You can use them later when you are both alone. Men adore the chicks in the magazines, but they will never approach a woman who looks like an angry bulldog. And a smile will show him that you definitely have interest.

**Look into his eyes**

This is the oldest way to show someone that you like him. Do not hesitate to seek contact with his eyes. And that is what men also seek.

**No questions**

Take your time asking the question, "What do you do?" Be interested in his work, not the money he receives for it. You can find other topics for conversation.

**Be positive**

Nobody likes frowning and forever dissatisfied women. Do not complain that the place is crowded, hot, unventilated, cold, etc. There are many positive topics for discussions. Music, movies, concerts, and so on.

Maybe you don't feel terrific. Probably you have gained some weight and also there might be an accumulated pressure, so it's no wonder that you don't feel like the most beautiful or the most attractive woman in the world. Calm down and relax. With a few small steps you will raise your confidence, have power, and be willing to experience unforgettable moments.

**Be in shape**

Not with a diet. Stringent restrictions will only make you more touchy and starvation has not helped anyone. Take up a sport. Don't pretend that there's still plenty of time before summer. If you walk three times a week, one month is sufficient to get in shape and the reflection in the mirror will make you smile. You like yourself, don't you?

**Take care of your body**

Start sleeping sufficiently. Sleeping well will best restore the power and the freshness of your face and body. Sleeping enough is essential if you want to look good.

Change your food system and take advantage of the huge abundance and diversity of fruits and vegetables.

Pamper yourself with a massage or procedure in a salon. This will increase the hormones of happiness. When you are happy you look beautiful!

## Underline your advantages

It's useless to focus on your shortcomings, or more precisely what you think is a disability. Nobody is perfect, so boldly underline those parts of your body that you find most attractive. You know how to do this, right? If you hesitate then ask somebody for advice.

## Surround yourself with mystery

If you are alone and you have decided to go hunting for a man, do not overact with sincerity. Don't openly infest the object of your desires; instead, stay a little mysterious. Men are hunters by nature, so let them go hunting. But if you already have a partner, come up with something crazy. Separate him from monotony and remind him of the first days of your relationship when the passion was much stronger.

## Take a course in massage

You will make him the luckiest man in the world. Light massage combined with appropriate music and aromas will unlock rusty passion.

## Indulge your instincts

Stop at least a week to comply with stereotypes. Even if you don't have luck with love as much as you want, relax and let yourself be wild and mad for a while. Sing on the streets, bathe during the night in the pool or the sea, buy a large straw hat and glasses. It definitely will attract the male looks and stress will give way to positive emotions.

## Be unpredictable

Men are scared of women who are unpredictable, but at the same time they are attracted to them. The hunter fights for its prey. And the loot is you. Run, but be sensible. Give him the opportunity to catch you and never lose you.

## Beware

Be crazy, but be reasonably crazy. Don't forget to use condoms and never forget them at home. Be sexy but don't be demonstratively sexy. Being sexy does not mean that you should look like a porn star. There are many small gestures that men find for irresistible. Here are some non-sexual gestures that arouse men.

Men are excited by women who:

- Drink beer by the bottle or smoke weed. But don't get it wrong by emulating masculine behavior (such as profanity). "What really turns me off is a woman who swears like a sailor" is what most men tell me.
- Play a sport (mainly because of the concentration sports require, and because of the shaking form of the body).
- Use lipstick. The movement of the lips during application makes them want to take the place of the lipstick. However, this must be the only beauty procedure that men must see. Masks and hair removal are private.
- Women who fix their hair. Putting up a pony tail, carelessly running your fingers
- through your hair—these things impress men.
- Women who lick their lips—again—out of bed. Licking of lips leads to drying and cracking, but occasionally you can afford it to attract his attention. To prevent cracking of your lips, use luster afterward.
- Women who smile shyly. As I already said, the "angry bulldog"-type women look good only in magazines. In reality, men like women who smile coyly.
- Women who pin their high-heeled boots. It's very nice that men are impressed by such things.

4

And there are men who like women who park their car between two other cars. Impressive, huh?

Sexy looks, great hair, and thick lips—do you think that all this is enough to make a man want you? Not only once, but every time? And not only in his bed, but throughout life in general? Think often about how you look, about your vision, and then you will have better chances with men. If you have corrupted teeth, bad breath, or if you look negligent, what man would pay attention to you?

The perfect appearance is not always sufficient to cause a man to fall in love with you. Men know what they want, so you should try to meet their taste. Here are some examples of how to go about it:

- **Be independent.** It is high time to learn to cope alone. Women who rely primarily on themselves have irresistible force to attract the strong sex. The role of the girly whimper discourages them, especially if it is combined with a constant search for the "perfect half" and frenzied desire for marriage.

- **Give him freedom.** You should let him do his favorite things that he has done before knowing you. And leave him to breathe from time to time; the relationship can not be twenty-four hours a day. If you don't agree with this, he will be quickly bored of you and will want to be free again. Create constantly interesting and exciting things for him and he will actually relinquish some old habits gradually. When you give him freedom he eventually will renounce it and be available all day for you. But be careful, because too much freedom means vacuity. Nobody said it is easy. Do not stick to your beloved and discreetly remind him about your feelings toward him. He should know that you care without constant prowl. Precisely measure the amount of freedom.

- **Ensure him peace.** Most men argue that women are not able to control. One of the biggest nightmares for men are the inconsolable female jealousy and the unsubstantiated female crying for no apparent reason. However, men are less quick-witted and forget about your monthly cycle. Better get out of your favorite dramatic role and try to be calm. And stop playing a cop—no one will partner the good cop in interrogation.

- **Share his interests.** Each representative of the strong sex

5

would like to share his interests with his favorite person. Imagine this: you both sit on the couch at home and scream for your team who scored a goal. Guarantee that he will fall in admiration. Also, you will expend a little negative energy. Besides, what prevents you from going with him to the gym or learning to snowboard? In all cases, physical activity is useful for a great figure. However, don't push for something that you don't like and don't find interesting. This will only worsen things. If you are interested in any sport, just reveal it to him. He could share your interests.

- **Curiosity.** It's an inherited feature for women to be curious but do not think that only women have this quality. Men don't like women to be curious. They get peeved and make unequivocal remarks. At the same time, they burn from curiosity. If you are curious and surely want to know something, act on it discreetly without irritating him. Do it using the small secrets that always help. When you learn the hot story don't turn it into gossip. This may cause harm.

- **Sexuality.** Do not think that your partner should always begin the love game. Also, don't think that it should run every time in the same way. Remember that there must be permanent effort which should come from both sides. Love is a long game, and it better be funny. Men also have their sexual fears, so help them. Create the appropriate love atmosphere. Be sure that you can do it because women are magicians. Be a little impromptu, provide good wine, and use gentle touches and kisses—all of that will set him up for the appropriate wave and then you will indulge in sensual sex. Forget the floodgate in terms of sex. Keep it open in the bedroom. Most men dream about open behavior during sex but they will never confess that they like it this way. The truth is that they approve of the innovative initiatives of women. No man can remain indifferent to the sexual frenzy of a woman.

# The Perfect Man: Hunting for Him

*A*t the beginning of each new relationship, women dream it will be the last one. They hope to have found one who—you know: the wedding dress, the children, and the understanding family. All we want is to have children and a good family, but how to prevent from making those errors after which come the disappointment, the separation (in worst cases, divorce), and all the things from the "dark side of love"? The most important thing is to listen to your voice. If anything is telling you that things will not be right, better end it as soon as possible, even if it is painful. Later it will hurt even more.

Don't think that great sex means perfect relations. If you don't get along in bed, this is not the man for you. Even if you want to change things, you will never succeed. If a communication between you is missing, know that there is no relationship. He is not the one for you. It is a mistake when sexual interest is assumed as love. Sex delivers joy to both partners but except sensual gratification nothing else connects them. Love is a sacrament, a storm of emotions, tenderness, consideration, mutual understanding, and mutual concern. Here are several signs that your relationship is not running:

"Today I don't want to see you, but tomorrow I will want to see you." This type of strong emotional relationship may be interesting for a while, but it will not give the security that you need. The good moments in a "normal" relationship must exceed the bad. If meetings are canceled more than held, things are not good. How ongoing are your conversations? Did you succeed in reaching a unanimous decision about what to do on Friday night, which movie to watch, or where to go for the weekend? Or at any time did you fight with teeth and claws for your wishes? If your view of spending time together is too different, it will create tension between you, because one of you will never be satisfied. It's better for both of you to find people closer to your sentiments. Don't stick for a man just because you don't want to be alone.

This is useless. There is a danger in getting used to the wrong guy, because then it will be very difficult to leave him. And most importantly, you are denying the opportunity to meet and win the better man. Sometimes in long-term relationships people need to rest from one another. However, when this need appears even during the first month, it is clear that rest and separation is the best treatment. Often in such relationships, splitting from many "rests," sex is the leading force, so you should be realistic. Some women are willing to endure terrible terms only to "maintain" a relationship. "Fight me, I love you." This is not the way to keep a man. No, no, and no. If he treats you like a princess at one time, but at others like a doormat; or if he tries to strike you, you should immediately discontinue the relationship and if necessary call the police.

In order to make the relationship genuine and complete, it should give you happiness and security, not fear and tears. And do not forget that the world has six billion people, half of whom are men. The real man is out there. Do not waste time with dimmed images. Be sure that sooner or later you will find exactly who you need and who will deserve you. Every woman dreams of a great love with whom to spend her life. The more the years pass with promiscuous relationships, the more you realize that you need someone special with whom you can build your future.

When the relationship with your guy begins to grow, start making more serious plans for your life. Usually the priorities that you had in your teenage years are very different from those that you have now at a later stage. When you are at the age of seventeen or eighteen, you are enjoying the wild love, the charming appearance, and the funny and enjoyable times spent together.

Once, however, you grow and start thinking of marriage, the above factors are more like a nice addition to the core requirements that the man next to you should own. It's clear that if you are still looking for a serious partner, it will be a little easier because now you know what kind of a man you want and if he does not meet the criteria you will just not fall for him. This can not be executed as a textbook, but when you become more mature, you can control with whom to create serious relationships and with whom not to.

However, there is another situation: when you realize it's time to take the next step with your longtime, but not-too-serious, relationship. For some, it may be coexistence; for others, a wedding; for another, a child; yet another—all of these things. You love him very much; you spend good time together and have great sexual life. The days during you were together were moments when you were most happy in life. And now comes the time to take a serious step. Then you become fearful and start to wonder: "Is he the man of my life? Is he the right for me?"

If you fall into this dilemma, here are a few answers to questions:

- **Does he have a serious job and is he responsible for it?** This is very important to know whether you can count on this man. However, he must be aware that he will be your mainstay and one day will have to resist you and your children. A man who does not bother to remain idle, is not a very reliable husband.
- **Does he think about the future or live day to day?** The adventurous spirit is a huge plus, but not all women like an adventure lifestyle. It's not good to commit to a man who lives day to day, who does not contemplate how he spend his money, and does not think about tomorrow when today is a good day.
- **Do you quarrel often?** Harmony is very important for living together. It is not possible not to fight, but scandals should not be a way of life. The more time spent together, the more the hassle will escalate and in one moment you may regret bitterly your choice.
- **Does he drink a lot?** It sounds naive, but never seriously bind with someone who has problems with alcohol and does not realize that he must stop drinking. I do not talk about those who like to sip, but rather of the men whose greatest weakness is the cup and for whom drink can make them unrecognizable. If your partner falls in this category you should decide whether you want such man. Otherwise, in time you may be a wife of an alcoholic and have serious problems because the passion for alcohol has increased over the years.
- **Does he respect you?** Old people say that after a while love goes away, and only respect remains. While it is good to look more optimistic and believe that after years the love can still remain strong, the respect that you receive from your

partner must be a leading criteria for you when you are taking a serious step in your relationship. It is very important whether your lover respects you, complies with your wishes, always stands by your side, and keeps your confidences. Remember that deciding how a man respects a woman depends on her. You are the one who "dictates" how he should behave with you.

- **Do you have a good sexual life?** Usually, sex between two people becomes better with time. However, if you have several years together and you no longer feel a sexual appetite for your partner, do not think that over time it will be fine. Do not be like the women who bind to a man and argue for their ease. It really is not the most important thing, but a good sex life is the basis of cordial relations between the two partners.

These are the most fundamental questions you should answer when you are contemplating a serious step with someone. If you still roam between the pros and cons, do the following: close your eyes, imagine life in twenty years and see whether he is there. If you are not quite sure, then give yourself more time to think and be completely secure in the correct answer. If, however, you feel that a lifetime would not be enough to enjoy one another and, despite his shortcomings, he is the perfect mate then nothing can wait. Life is too short to wait for the perfect people and the perfect moments. They may never appear...

If you dream of meeting your perfect half, do not wait and come out to look carefully and make your own choice. If you have decided to find the true love, then you should spend some time to meet him. It will not be easy, but here are a few landmarks to start. And remember everything is in your hands, including wardrobe, hair, and body language. You know that love is a special chemical reaction between two people, but there must be a catalyst to make it happen. Select the kind of the guy that you like most, and see where you can find them most often.

- **The athletic stallion.** He is the muscular male transmission of power, energy, and endurance. It's hard to resist them. The list is quite long with such guys. But where to find yours? Where else will you meet him, if not in the gym? Ask one athletic guy to help you with the weights or show you any exercise. This way you will attract his attention and raise his ego. The greatest benefit is for you—not only can you meet your partner in the hall, but also you will get in good shape and meet interesting people. You can easily make new contacts on the ski track, on a walk in the mountains, or near the swimming pool. Just smile and the conversation will be fine.

- **The curious cutey.** He is educated and intelligent; dress standard for his convenience and desire to learn new things constantly. Look in any bookstore, take in a new exhibition, visit the library or museums. The last two apply with full force if you are in a new location, such as at work or on a trip. Try to find him in theatrical productions and films. It is true that in the salon it is more difficult to talk to someone, and you can have a place among women. But at the end of the show calmly discuss it with some nice man. In this category are men who work in the field of high technology. It is easier to meet them through a computer network than in person. They are usually never away from their laptop, which sometimes prevents them from communicating fully. They are fed with information on any topic and have unlimited opportunities to find answers to any question. However, this should not discourage you, especially if you are interested in technological toys. Ask them everything; they will be happy to explain and their explanation will be very accurate.

- **The artistic type.** He is the individualist who will be easy to recognize in the crowd. He is characterized by a distracted look, and especially by his special fashion style and with slightly negligent look. You can meet him in stylish restaurants, galleries, exhibitions, theaters, cinemas, and more. The photographers do often walk on the streets hoping to catch a particular moment. For musicians it is clear—clubs. Keep in mind that artistic men live in their own world and ordinary flirtation is not always successful. You must be original and creative in order to catch the attention of such guy. Since a lot of them are very emotional, you have to pat their senses. And with these senses they feel the whole world around them.

- **The fashion-icon type.** He is financially stable and likes to demonstrate this. He is always in step with fashion, is vain, and is very funny in a boyish way. You can see him in the most refined restaurants, clubs, and bars. He often goes in the beauty salons for a new haircut, manicure, and massage. In addition, you can find him in the fashion boutiques, where he spends large amounts of money. Of course, he keeps in good shape in the gym. To impress him, you should be not only stylish but also modern. It is not necessary to dress expensively, but something from a famous brand will definitely impress him.

- **The successful strategist.** He has worked a lot and has achieved even more. He has his own style and exquisite taste in everything. He likes good food and quality drinks. He is able to rest efficiently. This type of man is usually thirty-plus years old and has a hobby, to which he devotes his free time. They are fans of the noble sports such as tennis, riding, pool, and more. They like high-speed and new experiences. Therefore you can meet them in a variety of places and their stylish appearance can be seen from afar. They attend required restaurants with their own traditions and elegant clubs and bars. They love the major sports centers and stores. It is not necessary to dress glamorously to impress them. It is sufficient to be sincere and a little romantic—the successful man does not like games and respects the individual look.

Choose your prince. And do not forget that he is not your savior who will defend you from everything. Today he is your sole and equal partner. He is the prince of your dreams but in the modern variant. And you are an amazing creature full of new ideas and wishes who deserves to be happy. If he realizes that then you have found the perfect man for you. On your way to your favorite it is likely you will meet new friends, so do it! You will not lose anything and will only win. Men are not "goods" that you can buy. But let's try. Here are the basic rules of shopping for men:

- **Be flexible.** Why limit yourself with only men who fulfill your ideals? You know how it happens sometimes: a shirt, which does not appear right on the rack, turns out to be perfect on you. It is the same with men. Give them a chance; do not reject them because their eyes are parti-colored and not brown.

- **Do not blindly follow fashion, especially when you are looking for something more than a one night stand.** Don't choose only on appearance. The most terrible thing is to spend your life with a handsome but boring man. You would not take a dress that does not allow you to breathe, right? If you should choose between the handsome and the entertaining, select the second. Then you will be grateful.

- **Shop in your favorite places.** As with shopping in real life, the most important thing in shopping for men is the overall experience. You should feel at home to show the best of yourself. Go to places where you feel nice even in your own company. None of us likes to go into stores with dour saleswomen. When you are in your favorite place you will express a positive mood and that will attract men's attention.

- **Pick your friends.** It may sound nasty, but you should have friends for all occasions. For the purposes of shopping for men, you should have a friend who can give you courage to take the first step, if necessary. In no case should you go out with women who only criticize others and are in a bad mood all the time. Even if the "little prince" invites them to a date, they will still be unsatisfied.

- **Recall your secret capacity.** Remember all those signals of your body that men find breathtaking.

- **Manage your voice.** Voice control is important, always and everywhere. Talking too quietly or yelling will not reflect well on your ability to communicate. Look the one that you want in his eyes and then smile to him. If he smiles in response, you will have a new acquisition. If not, then you better give up.

# How to Attact His Attention

One of the most difficult things in relationships is the beginning. Do not be one of those women who starts watching the ceiling when the man they like passes by. Also don't behave like a clown to attract his attention. If you do these tricks he will look at you scornfully and mockingly. It's better you try other ways to catch his attention.

- **Smile at him.** Wherever you meet him—at the bar, in the store, or on the street—the easiest way to show him that you are not indifferent, is to smile. If he smiles back, the beginning is set!
- **Be amusing**—but not funny. Come up with some amusing (but not insulting) comment on one of your friends or a situation you were in—at a party, in a shop queue, at the checkout, or in the office restroom. If nothing suitable comes to mind, better go back to the first trick.
- **Search for help.** Men like to feel strong. Ask him to give you something from the top shelf in the store or to help you find the right room, street, fax paper, or whatever you need at the moment (if you don't need anything at the moment, think of something; he is your goal so be creative). Most men will be happy to help you. Having added your gratitude with a smile and a look in his eyes, you have a great chance for a next meeting.

# The Best Places to Meet the Man of Your Dreams

*T*he closed world at work and at home does not offer many opportunities to meet new people—including, possibly, the man of your life. The first and fundamental rule in the search for a man is to stop looking in a sense. Do not look at any new acquaintance as the potential father of your children. Relax, be glad of your autonomy and free time, and thicken them with engaging activities. Nobody knows where she will be surprised by love. If you are exhausted from ideas on how to fill your free time and how to find new friends, get inspiration from these suggestions:

- **Walk the dog in the park** (if you don't have a dog, now is the best time to get one). The dog is the best friend of the woman who has much free time and no friend. Get him in the park along with other lucky owners of dogs. The "dog" theme is suitable for starting a conversation with any animal lover. Furthermore, you will be sure that your new friends are not allergic to fur.

- **Take a course** (or how to combine the useful with the pleasant). Foreign languages, dances, martial arts—no matter what you choose, starting a course is a great way to diversify, to learn something new, and to meet people with similar interests to yours. If you choose martial arts, chances to impress the males of the group are greater because men are impressed by women who are interested in "male" activities.

- **Planes and trains.** Low-cost airline carriers have made the

17

trip by plane quite accessible. The only inconvenience is that you must often fly with transfer and spend several hours waiting at the airport. But while you wait, you could meet him. Waiting for a plane (or train or bus) is another way to talk to a man. You will make your waiting less annoying and also will increase the chance next time of not traveling alone. As for cars, riding on a stop for a woman who is alone is not recommended.

- **Flights by wings of music.** Attending a concert can be a ticket to your love. Fan sites are also a convenient place to talk, and why not to meet people with similar musical interests?

- **Online dating.** The Internet is the most popular place for making contacts. When you do not see the person in front of you it is much easier to say what you think, to ask very personal questions, or to share your fantasies. The Internet is where you can lead an active social life without even leaving home.

- **Sports.** First, they're good for your health and figure. And second, there are enough men who also run in the morning or go to the gym. And to drink a cup of tea or a coffee after exhausting workout in pleasant company is a proposal that's hard to resist.

- **Have dinner out.** Convert the crowded restaurant into your ally. Go out to dinner alone; there is nothing wrong with it. Remember that not only single women have dinner out, but also single men. Even if you do not meet the love of your life in any of these places, you will certainly find new friends.

# How to Seduce Him

*Y*ou have already chosen your goal. Will he notice you? How to attract his attention? What to do to show him that you unambiguously like and desire him? How to awake his passion? Here are a few small female secrets, which no man can resist:

If you're in a restaurant, but you're at different tables:

- Start talking louder or laugh openmouthed. It is true that such behavior is scorned and considered low, but this is the only way to catch his attention. But don't go too far otherwise he will deem you frivolous and ill-mannered. If he looks at you reproachfully, smile at him and in return he will smile back. Watch him for a while. When a woman does not stop looking at a man it becomes clear that she wants to make a contact with him. At the moment he see you, revoke your eyes. Repeat this two or three times. On the fourth turn, let him capture your eyes and stay with crossed eyes for a few seconds; then shyly look somewhere else. The fifth time, smile at him! After some minutes a waiter will bring you a glass of wine and will explain that "the gentleman from the next table wishes you a good time tonight!" If after this gesture of attention, the "gentleman" does not come to sit at your table, do not despair! Go to the bathroom and when you return pass along his table. Drop your lipstick from your purse—he will leap from his seat and rush to you to pick it up. Stop, but do not bend down. Let him closely examine your body when he lifts your lipstick from the ground. The lipstick is appropriate for the case because it is small and when he give it to you, you will inevitably touch his hand. You will both feel the gentle touch. Slightly bend down your head and start moving your eyelids to show him that you are excited, then thank him for the kind gesture and invite him to be your company until the end of the evening!

If you're in a restaurant and sit at one table:

- Take the cup with both hands, start to caress it, and finally pass your forefinger on the edge of it. Slightly bend your head and start looking at him with a seductive, warm, and inviting look. Let your lips be slightly opened. For the next step, moisten your lips with tongue, but do not lick them!
- Play with your hair! It certainly will suggest that you like him and want to look good, and he will notice that you feel worried and excited. Men like to keep the situation under control. Therefore, roll a lock with your finger and then let it open as falling in his arm! Bend slightly forward and he will look into your neckline. Do that pretending that you do not notice and he will assess that you are tactful. Just be careful not to overdo it! Every gesture of yours should look childlike and spontaneous!
- With an amused look, with one hand grab a finger on the other and start playing with it. This again shows discomfort, but in this gesture there is some coquetry.
- Go to the bathroom to get right your makeup. Certainly, he will follow you with his eyes. Take advantage of the case; walk gently and sway your thighs. He will notice not only your fine shape, but also that many other men are looking at you. He will feel satisfied that you are with him and not with another guy—you will be his trophy! And that is exactly what you want, isn't it!?
- When you return from the bathroom, look only at him and smile. Sit down and renew your conversation as if you never felt that the eyes of all men have been directed at you. This will show him that you care only for him and nobody else. This way you will raise his confidence and dignity.

If you are at work:

- Arrange somehow to travel alone together in the elevator. When the door opens and he lets you come out first, walk by close to him as if there is not enough space. Let him notice your scent. Call him to help you with your computer and when you start to explain what is wrong, "accidentally" touch his hand, which has propped up on your desk. Then when he begins to use the mouse, put your hand on his hand. After that, apologize and blush innocently.
- Stretch on the chair and give yourself a look of satisfaction from well-finished work. Once you catch his attention and he looks at you, smile guiltily with a look asking for understanding.
- While both of you are waiting for the coffee machine, confess to him that since you are alone, you do not sleep well at night and feel tired.
- Get ready to go home, and when you see that he also is preparing to leave, follow him! You will be together in the elevator and will talk until you reach your cars, and if you go by public transportation, he probably will propose to drive you.
- If you lunch together, order a salad that has celery and seafood, and for dessert, chocolate ice cream! This is a real aphrodisiac! He will definitely be impressed!
- Go to the file cabinet to find documents you need. Reach for the top shelves and while you stretch, he will have time to inspect and admire the fine curves of your silhouette. Pretend you don't know he is looking at you. Then ask him for help because you can not reach a document. Use the trick of dropping all the files on the floor. It will be a great pleasure for him to help you pick them up and then rearrange them.

If you're on the street:

- At the moment you feel that he looks at you, gently raise your skirt, ostensibly to get more easily on the sidewalk.
- When he is coming against you, wait for the time of

divergence and then trip. Fall right into his embrace. Say: "Thank you! You have saved my life!" And then ask him for a coffee to attest your gratitude!

- In the queue for sandwiches, ask him to hold your envelope for a while so you can get money from your purse, in which you never find what you seek.
- Take his place when you are on the queue and buy the newspaper that you want. Tell him that you are in a rush and that's why you have taken his place on the queue. By doing this you will catch his attention and it is possible that you travel together—here is an appropriate moment for apology.
- It is raining buckets. He stops a taxi. Get up first. Tell him with a smile: "Do not stand in the rain! The taxi will drive you first and then me!" If you like unengaged men, you may not come home until the morning. If he did not gather enough courage, at least you know where he lives!

# *Convert to a Dream Woman*

*T*here is a huge difference between what women think men want from them and what men really want from women. Here are characteristics of the "dream woman":

- **She has her own life.** Take care of yourself. Follow your own way of life. Do not forget your friends and family and do not fully devote yourself to your new boyfriend. It is not easy, because all women do precisely this; their world is running low with him and that is at least choking. In time, women think of themselves and fall into the other extreme: they forget about their relationship because they want to catch up on all the things that they have sacrificed. So do not make meaningless sacrifices and have your own life.
- **She is sexy without being obtrusive.** Clothing is just a part of being sexy. Men like big necklines and short skirts, it is a fact, but only as a background. If you want him to take you seriously, do not overdo it with sincerity in dressing. Being sexy does not mean only showing your natural parts. The overall vision is what drives men wild. The behavior is the other part of being sexy, and most women are overactive. When you like a man, do not try to choke him with your breast. Most men hate that. If you are at the beginning of your relationship they prefer not to immediately have a sexual contact with you. A tender touch on the shoulder, a quick touch of his feet under the table, holding gaze for saying "hi" a few seconds more than the normal—these are gestures to show a man that you are interested in him

without being intrusive. If your relationship becomes deeper and you are already together for sure, you can afford small hot-teasers in public places

- **She waits awhile before sex.** Sex is no longer a taboo topic, and intimate relationships are a big step for all couples. Most women do not even realize that sex changes the dynamics of the relationship. If you have sex with him too early you will think that the relationship is very serious, which will not be true because feelings need time to deepen.

- **She can be his best friend.** Support him in important moments. Be sure he understands your support and appreciates your gestures.

- **She will never push him.** This is one of the most important things. Men have congenital hatred for all kinds of pressure. Avoid calling him a thousand times a day, sending him too many e-mails, or making plans for your future in ten years. Men do not like to feel involved. They just want to enjoy the fact that they are with the woman they love.

- **She does not allow him to behave badly with her.** Men do not respect women who accept any behavior from anyone. If he knows that he can not behave with you as it occurs to him, he will respect you more. This not only applies to your boyfriend but also to all people around you.

# First Date: The First Mistake? Stop It!

After a certain amount of time being single, an invitation for coffee or beer after work by a colleague looks like the chance of your life. This might be true, since you can never know when and where you will meet the love of your life. But often women, mostly from excitement, manage to turn off their colleague so he may never think of a second date. Too personal—the invitation for coffee is not a proposal of marriage. Women tend to overstate the meaning of words, gestures, and events. So when he invites you for a coffee, try not to be too excited and don't think about the white dress and the flowers; just go to drink a coffee. Do not rush into serious talks of life, do not complain of ex-boyfriends, do not share your problems, much less reveal feelings, emotions, and sexual thoughts that he has provoked in you. Just spend a pleasant afternoon with someone and enjoy the time to talk and not to pour out your soul. Only time will show whether anything will happen.

- **Mistake No. 1:** She hasn't seen and she hasn't heard. Another problem is that women do not accept people as they are. In order not to be disappointed after a while, listen and watch carefully. The man always reveals himself with what he says and does. Pay attention to how he looks and what he says. Does he mention his ex-girlfriends and parents? Does he complain about his boss or talk about future creative plans? All these things will show you what kind of a person stands in front of you—a real vision, not a phony image of a prince.

- **Mistake No. 2:** Don't be the drowning man who caught a straw. This is the biggest mistake of all. Many women think the relationship is what will fix their lives and seek it out like a life preserver. Rather, the relationship should complement your already beautiful life. Do not think that if you have a boyfriend, things will be much different. Actually, they will not be different. With a boyfriend it is more fun, more sexual, and more relaxing, but not much different from the usual. Get out, have fun, flirt, have reasonable sex and the relationship will come when you least expect it.

# *Several Ways to Seduce Him before the Others Do*

*I*magine that in your office a new and attractive colleague has been hired. Even before he starts, you and your colleagues have already developed a crush on him. The problem is that you are not the only one who wants him. What to do in order to catch him?

**Be the first.** This is the easiest way to get a few steps ahead of the competition. The latecomers are always satisfied with the crumbs.

**Estimate the competition.** The battle is always won more easily when you emphasize your strength against the weakness of your opponents. Be sly and lead the battle only when it is worth it and makes sense.

**Be different and unique.** If you can not be the best in one category, be the best in another. You can easily defeat competition by being wittier, more amiable, stronger, more confident, more impassioned, and a better listener. It is clear that the more talented you are and the more qualities you have compared to others, the better your outcome.

**Do not pay attention to your opponents.** Be above them. If you can not fight against them with class, you better not start to compete. Have integrity and dignity.

**Defend yourself.** Be prepared for hostile attacks. Some people earn as ruin everything that others have achieved. Be prepared. If you want others to respect you, you must first respect yourself and resist with dignity all verbal attacks and petty intrigues.

**Make good unions.** Surround yourself with friends to build more support and, of course, establish protection against those who hate you. And it is quite likely that you will take your desired man's heart more quickly with the help of your faithful friends. Furthermore, it is always better when there is someone to back you up. All men and women know how to read the signals of the opposite sex so you should participate in the game as everyone else. Men do not like overbearing women, but somehow you should show him that you are interested in him. Be a secret attacker.

**Be around him and then hide.** The more contact you have with someone and give him a chance to know you, the more likely he will like you. Find reasons to spend more time together. Ask him to help you with something, pretend that you are looking for something in the same room, and so on. When you notice that he has become accostomed to your company, hide yourself. Do not be always available for him; show him that you have many other interests besides him. In this way he, will impatiently wait the time when you will be free, and while waiting, he will only think—about you.

**Do not do nice things for him. Let him do nice things for you.** When you have feelings for someone it is quite normal that you will want to to do something nice for him. Do not smother him with gifts; this is the male part of the game. Let him bring you a coffee or something to eat if you work together. Allow him to be cavalier, he will assess your gesture.

**Look at him.** Playing eye games to attract a mate is as old as the world. Crossed eyes signify for men and women that there is chemistry between them. Lovers elicit strong gazes from one another, but pay attention the time because it is extremely inappropriate to be looking at someone and neglect everything else around you. To maintain a balance between manners and flirting, apply the following tactics: When you are with company and someone speaks, look at the speaker, as is appropriate to do when someone talks to you. At the end of the speech turn your eyes to the object of desire and keep your eyes on him a little more than normal. By this way he will know that you are interested in him and it is his views on the issue that you comment.

**The secret of the expanded pupils.** In no case should you resort to medicine to expand your pupils; instead, use the "darkest" moments as much as possible. Men find a woman more attractive if her pupils are expanded. For the same reason, romantic dinners are with candles. Not only because the scarce light hides the features, but also because the pupils widen. As you are already attracted by the man, pupils will widen every time you look at him. So benefit from the moments when you look at him with all your love. If the object of your desire remains insensitive to you after the implementation of all these tricks, just accept that and realize that it is not meant to happen. Keep your dignity and do not jump on him as an animal. Men do not like invasive women. Wish him a happy life in your mind and move on. There is no sense in fighting for lost causes.

# *Five Great Ways to Get Noticed*

*G*etting a man to pay attention to you is the key to a successful night out. But how to get five, ten, or one hundred people to notice you, even for a few seconds?

It is not as difficult as it seems; simply launch the secret weapons in the right time.

- **Come in memorably.** No, do not intentionally try to fall, to give a push, or to pour a drink on someone. When you go into a club or a party, stand at the entrance with your most wonderful posture, straighten up your arms, lightly lift your chin, and look at all the people who are there. Wait for one of your friends to notice you, and rush over to them. By doing this you will allow the people who have seen you enter the opportunity to see who you are with, where you will sit, and all those little details that will help the person that likes you to come to you and to start talking to you.
- **Look memorable.** Think of your own fashion signature, which can differ from the crowd. A scarf, a hat, sunglasses, belt, shoes—anything that is just yours and with which you can appear everywhere, so in time people will remember you. Just do not overdo it with too many accessories. The combination of sports hat, sunglasses and high-heeled shoes will make you look like a freak and not marvelous.
- **Talk memorably.** All people are interested in the latest gossip. However, I don't talk about ugly stories that could

ruin the prestige of a person, but rather about the curious details of life that not everybody knows. Read news about show business; there is no one who is not interested in the life of celebrities. When you have a similar story to tell, your listeners will become friendlier. Forget nasty stories about lovers, stuff from work, bad habits, or ridiculing anyone.

- **Communicate memorably.** Make the guests at the party talk about you as you think up an interesting way to introduce yourself to the people. A famous Hollywood actress at the beginning of her career got a role in a movie, just by asking the guests at the party not for their names, but rather where they grew up and what their dreams were when they were children, thus impressing everyone. Do something like that and in minutes everybody will know you.

- **Leave the party memorably.** Not on four legs—no. Do you remember the story of Cinderella? She left first and then she married the prince. Do you know why? She stayed at the party long enough to be noticed and before overdoing the cocktails. This of course is just a joke, but the look of a drunken woman is not very pleasant and you should keep yourself from drinking too much. Leaving the party is another great occasion to talk one more time with the person who hasn't stopped looking at you the whole night. And he can offer to send you somewhere.

# *Squash the Competition*

*Y*ou are already together. He, of course, is the personification of everything that you want from a man. Perfect. However, it is very likely that many other women will find him just as perfect and will not hesitate to take him from you. Here are some ideas on how to deal, in a civilized and mature manner, with the competition:

- **Be positive.** You may feel a bit down every time an attractive and assuming woman that he knows greets you with the most artificial smile in the world. Instead of showing that you don't like her, smile at her. Be polite with her and remember that you are the one with whom he will be at home tonight. Furthermore, men are irritated from unreasonably jealous women. And making a problem from a mere smile is really stupid.
- **Watch the women who pass by you.** You should accept that men are looking at other women. They do this not because they want to leave you, but because of the nice view. It is the same as going to a gallery; you look at all the pictures but you buy only one of them. Join him in watching and commenting on these women. Just refrain from bitter remarks, because your man will decide that you are jealous and will begin to tease you—just to see how you get angry for nonsense. Men are like that and you should accept it.
- **Remind him of yourself.** If he speaks for more than ten minutes with a female friend (and you are sure she does not want merely to be his friend), then you can do the following: take his hand, kiss him gently on the cheek, and say that

you'll be back shortly. You will show the woman that you are really together. Furthermore, the physical contact will remind him that he is not alone and that he has overdone the conversation. In no case should you dash out, stomp your leg, make faces, or insist like a little child that you leave immediately. He will become nervous and she will exploit the situation to present herself in the best light. You do not want that, right?

The competition slowly builds their tactics, using the weaknesses of your partner. The non-standard women are the most dangerous rivals; they do not look like seducers. Usually they wear skirts around the knee and do not seem to flirt. However, it is possible for you to experience a real anger toward this ordinary woman. Also you will not believe that this woman can be interesting to men.

The woman of your nightmares may look to your friend too innocent or too wrinkled. Or even boring or indifferent. Even though he assures you that he is not interested in her, you will probably suspect that this creature is about to snatch your man. However, pull out your concerns; the man next to you would feel insulted by your hysterical behavior. He can even advise you to take leave because you look tired or he can justify your behavior with complexes. He may also yell at you or sink into gloomy silence. It is clear you can not handle jealousy. However, it is enough to find the weaknesses of your rivals. These tips will help you to escape with dignity from the unpleasant situation.

According to their capacity, these rivals come in several types:

- **The Little One.** This rival can unexpectedly turn out to be your sixteen-year-old niece. You are resentful that this little lady too often grabs her uncle in hand, sits on his knee, and blushes at his compliments. If you announce that this young lady flirts with him you will only get in trouble.

   **Advice.** Among all the rivals, this type is the least harmful. In most cases her flirtation will not grow into something substantial. Do not show that you accept her as a rival. Treat her like a little kid. You can even advise her to change the color of her lipstick. Tell her your good recommendations only in the presence of your boyfriend or husband.

- **The Mature One.** The image of a mature, experienced, and world-weary woman gives great freedom of action. She takes on the role of advisor and so she imputes suspicions of others. Having completely forgotten the "lady," she will easily afford more coquetry and frivolity.

**Advice:** Every morning and evening repeat to your guy that you dream of living to the age of this lady and to look as good as her. Do not worry that you will tire him of such stories. His boredom is a sign that you have removed her.

- **The Friend.** She has slept with him in a common tent, has saved him from many things, and has cried on his shoulder on campus. Maybe she alludes to you that she has had a relationship with your man or even that their relations remain.

  **Advice:** Do not start to panic. Most likely, his "friend" is convinced of love between them only in her head. The only thing that really connects her with your man are the common memories that happened ten years ago. Give her the opportunity to speak of them for hours, but only when your boyfriend is there and is listening. Continue to require new details. The stupid things from his youth will come out and he will be angry not only at himself but at his witness to his tempestuous boyhood.

# *Seduction Lessons*

*C*an you think of any woman who looks amazing in even the most awful dress? Or while dripping spaghetti sauce all over herself still appears charming and impressive? Being sexy is not just a defiant appearance. It's also a state of mind. In female nature there is the ability to provoke and seduce. You just have to improve this capability and turn it to quality. In this way you will learn how to manage much of the male world around you.

It is not necessary to be a lion tamer with whip in hand, no matter that many men are like wild animals. There is also no need to play the fatal woman if you don't want that. A few simple rules will help you to adjust to a heat wave.

- **Keep your mysterious halo.** Take your time to say and show everything; retain some secrets that will keep men on the alert. And not just them. It's not bad to have one more trump card hidden, and to use it when nobody expects it. This may be a hurriedly smile, a roguish look, or garters that stick out capriciously. And you may make a soft demonstration of some of your valuable qualities, for instance not spreading gossip of your colleague.
- **Show more self-esteem.** Saying "Yes" and agreeing with the fancies of your relatives and friends all the time is mediocre. And it is not sexy, especially if in a new relationship you adapt to your partner. That does not mean to behave badly and hostile toward all. Just do not agree with the others at your own expense. If you do not respect yourself, they will respect you less.
- **Be confident in yourself.** Some men really like slimy girls who constantly need a strong presence next to them.

Everyone has weaknesses and fears, but it is rather better to be a confident chick who knows what she wants and charges the parade. To play the role of a permanent victim is not sexy and quickly becomes annoying. It does not allow you to be an equal girlfriend, even less lover and partner. It is better to be strong and to control the situation.

The dramatic roles are for the cinema. Do not carry them into life; there is no place for them there. You do not need to have a schedule of your nervous bursts associated with the going out of your man. Nor harassing your girlfriend at night because you made a boob of yourself in the office or complaining that you have no time for a manicure. Before exaggerating the daily occurrences that even can not shake you, try to take deep breath and stop for a while. When you are more relaxed, look at things from another angle. Perhaps a more fun one.

Stop saying "I, I, I." You are not the center of the universe, or at least not for everyone. If you do not like your life and you are always dissatisfied with something, you are unlikely to have many friends. And conversation that's only about you is not very appetizing. Being kind to others and being interested in their lives is not a manifestation of weakness, but of attention. Hugs, light touching, and questions like "How was your day?" will make all around you seek your tender company.

Joking is not a crime. It is terrible to constantly remain silent and expect others to keep the talk going. It is not sexy, right? It is not a crime to share your views on any issues, or to have facetious humor and make others laugh. Using these tips it will be easier for you to successfully communicate in the office, with new people, and everywhere else. This is an internal sensation. To achieve it, you should like yourself primarily. The hot chicks usually are well aware of what they want, so become one of them! It is a miracle that men and women manage to keep in touch when they are so different from one another. Even in the moments when it is expected that they should reach full unity, they still have radically different notions of that how should things happen.

Three things that women can learn from men:

- Pictures of half-naked bodies can definitely arouse you.
- Enjoy the moment. Thinking about tomorrow's problems during sex will only ruin the experience.
- If you want sex, do not use oblique ways to show your desire. Be clear in your wishes and you will both win.

# The Differences between the Man Who is in Love and the Man Who Feels Only Passion

**B**etween the man who is in love and the man who feels only passion there is nothing in common, although in the early romantic relationship you can confuse yourself over both states. To avoid regrets, turn your attention to the ways in which they vary.

He is in love with you if:

- He assures you that you are more beautiful than all beautiful ladies taken together.
- He confesses that his previous relationships were not very successful.
- He praises qualities in you that nobody has so far noticed.
- He cares for your professional success.
- He writes down your phone number in three places and immediately remembers your birthday.
- He is excited before the first meeting of your relatives and friends.
- He carefully listens to your mother's story about your baby years.
- He invites you home, to show you his baby and pet pictures.
- He calls you with funny names.
- He sends you home no matter how late it is.
- He teaches you how to drive a car and how to catch fish.

- He sincerely is surprised that you have decided to lose weight.
- He does not care what his friends think about you.
- He takes advice from you about what suit to buy.
- He introduces you to all his married friends and even confesses that he envies that they are married.

He feels only passion if:

- He makes compliments that you have heard from others too.
- He thinks that he looks like a Hollywood star.
- He asks you of any potential rivals.
- He tells you with pleasure about his past relationships.
- He cannot remember the name of your mother and your favorite chocolates.
- He is interested only in the page of your album with pictures where you are grown.
- He invites you to his home, as he promises champagne, candles, and coffee in taste.
- He remembers the aroma of your perfume and the first three digits of your phone number.
- He gives reasonable advice for your appearance.
- He gets you in a taxi if the date goes on too long.
- He tells you in details what his friends think about you.
- He calls you a refined woman, the eighth wonder in the world, and the cat woman.
- He takes advice from you about what tie to wear to his boss's birthday party.
- He carelessly announces how much everyone values him at work, what automobile he will soon buy, and which islands he considers for the best holiday.
- He likes you to tell him gossip and interesting stories. When you start to talk about your troubles at work, he begins to yawn.

# The Bad Boys and Their Lies

Psychologists long ago defined the main qualities of the "bad boys," who become magnets for women even though it's for a short time. Here are some of the main characteristics of this type of man:

- They do not call during the week but they always call on Saturday night to invite you to a party.
- They do not apologize if they have forgotten about a date.
- They forget or do not know your birthday and other important dates.
- They openly flirt with other women when you are together.
- They call at 1 a.m. to tell you how much they miss you after they have been all night with another girl.
- At least once they have had a squabble with the police.

Despite all these shortcomings—or, more accurately, exactly because of them—the "bad boys" are so popular among women. In the mind of females all these features convert the bad boy to an attractive and sexy man.

That is why:

- It is never boring with him. He is improvident and exciting.
- He is strong, aggressive, and confident and that makes women feel cared for.
- Most women have never met someone else to make them feel more wanted.
- His failures in life are not his mistakes and he definitely tries to make things right.

- He is very charming and emotional.
- He constantly repeats how much he likes the girl next to him and that assures women that he really thinks what he says.
- He needs the woman to be around him.
- He never looks pitiful and unhappy.

Women are extremely happy when they have succeeded in catching the attention of a person like him. It is known that he could have every woman that he wanted and every woman would feel flattered that he has chosen exactly her. The combination of childishness and nastiness in the image of a "bad boy" is what attracts so many women. Such men can open all facets of a woman—the mother, the lover, and the friend. Rarely does such a relationship last long, but the bittersweet memory of him comes always again and again.

You know very well that to conquer females, men often hide the truth, go round the problems, jump over the sharp stones that hurt; they even lie about themselves. Here are the most charming men lies:

"This dress looks fabulous on you." "You are not fat." "You are a great cook." "I want to make you happy." "I would never sleep with a woman who I do not love." "When you are with me you will feel like a queen."

In every TV show the man begins with his favorite role. He takes the image of purity and virginity, without a past or experience. Before starting to flirt with you he will immediately convert himself to a shy guy who has dated only one or two women. Behind all this is hidden a thin game the purpose of which is to provoke compassion and warm feelings from the woman in order to win her. This way, without wasting too much effort, he can feed himself for a long time with the feelings of his compassionate woman. After that, many of the bad boys bite as vampires and suck out the emotional energy of their women for many years. The man who fascinates never risks ruining his image by listening to meaningless stories with no advantages for him. When the woman wants to talk with him, he goes out, finds urgent work at home, or starts to watch TV and says that he does not feel like talking right now. In the most difficult cases, he just becomes quiet and lets the problems resolve by themselves or—most often—by her.

Faithful to the principle "the silence is gold," the males have gone even further. They are quiet because that may cause them even small conflicts which will only bother them and they assume that the one who does not speak, does not tell lies. And when he should lie, it is to praise the woman's qualities. And again—for her good. There is no woman who won't be glad from the compliment "You are amazing!" or, "You are great in bed."

And the lies about being good in bed are their most used lies, because there is not a woman who will not be happy to hear that she is great in bed. When telling a woman that she is amazing, the men realize that they are making a compliment to the woman, but do not realize that they are telling a true lie. As for the women, there is not a woman who wants to be compared with another woman.

# Perfect Ideas to Make Him Want You to Faint

*C*an you think of any playful ideas to make a man want you so much that he will faint? I mean something more romantic. The romance is not an old-fashioned thing from your grandmother's time, when men gave women flowers on every date.

And men are not just sex-machines; they deserve a special attitude. They like naughty games, but this also becomes boring. You should know that what you think of as romantic is not always the same for your partner. And stop with the same old things; dinner with candles is very boring. Here are some ideas about how to change the tactic without becoming too tedious.

- **Notes and SMS.** Men are actually quite impressed by such banter. However, do not send him a message telling him what will happen tonight or what your underwear is. Just write that you think about him. Or that you have heard your favorite song and it reminded you of how you both have danced on it. The spontaneous thought for your friend will raise his confidence. You can use a mobile phone, e-mail, and instant messaging.

No matter how busy you are you can always send him an animated emoticon "kiss," for example. This will remove some of the tensions in the office for you and for him. If you leave for work before he does, leave him a note. Write him that you kiss him for good morning and wish him a good day. Leave a trace from you in the bathroom; perfume yourself there. Your beloved will assess the gesture.

- **Breakfast.** Your partner will be glad if you serve him breakfast in bed. Pamper him with his favorite dish—or a cup of aromatic coffee, if he has the harmful habit of not eating breakfast. Do not do this only on the weekends. If you are late for work one morning to have breakfast together, he will like this. And he probably prefers to have some time with you, so do not rush—enjoy your breakfast together.
- **Leisure.** His, of course. Try to add to his favorite diversion; the vast majority of men accept this gesture as very nice and romantic. Take your friend to a football game, learn how to ski together, or join that which gives him pleasure. Of course it should give pleasure to you too. There is no need to break your hand skating or to murmur that your manicure is damaged while bowling. And do not take it as an obligation—if you pout he will not be happy. Remember that your boyfriend likes to be spoiled as much as you do. Do not wait for him always to open the door in front of you.

# Temptations He'll Die For

*M*en also have secrets. Here are a few:

- Whisper to him that you are dying to have quick sex. First, it does not take long. Second, it provides an extremely stormy orgasm.
- Accidentally rub your breasts in his hand while passing by him at dinner or a family gathering.
- Tell him that you want to read his fortune, which is sometimes served with coffee. Whatever it says there, say "You will be very happy and very naked as soon as we get home."
- Carelessly flip the channels and stop when you reach the "you-know-what" channel.
- Show him your new necklace, without anything else on you.
- Challenge him to a competition called, "Who will do a better massage?"
- Take off his pants while he is talking on the phone.
- Show him that you want sex just before you go out to a formal dinner.
- When you send him to the store add on the list and "romantic" goods such as candles, strawberries, and champagne. He will understand what is on your mind.
- Classics: An oral "touch" in the car. Unsurpassed, especially if you do it suddenly, having previously held cold and arrogant.

# A Jolly Atmosphere: A Condition for Maintaining Good Relations

*W*hen defining the relationship with the word "boring," you can compare it to a building, slowly crumbling down—outside it looks great, but something has slipped out and no one can understand where it has vanished. Here, that "something" is the laughter. It disappears not on purpose, but because of oversight. You spend whole nights in silence. Even your sexual life ceases to be cheerful. Also you are rarely together and you do not laugh.

If you can see it coming in time, quickly try to avoid it before it is too late and your relationship is destroyed. The sunny atmosphere is the main condition for maintaining a good relationship. Partners who laugh together actually say, "I believe that you love me even when I am stupid." The joy of the joint life could easily be lost in today's complicated world, but it might come back if both partners make some effort. It does not even require much time—only mutual consent.

If your joint life is missing the atmosphere of joy, here are some tips that will help to return those lost delights:

- **Lower your level of mistrust.** Many couples believe that the joint life is something very serious: a joyless routine of paying loans, meetings, and other obligations. They have been always told that to create a family means no rest.

Work without rest and jokes makes your life boring, and this has an impact on your relationship. Thus the first step is to take some time off. Plan ease in your relations. Ease and plan are apparently two incompatible concepts, but you don't have to be childlike, if you do not have time.

Find time for yourself, forget all other duties and deal with what you want. Spend the day together, go out of town. Go to the zoo, buy balloons, feed the monkeys. A very busy man left for one night a week to spend the day with his wife. He hired a babysitter and never told his wife what his intentions were. Once he took her to the fair, another time to a concert. On a different occasion, he arranged dinner with candles. The main thing here is not where they were walking or what they did, but that it was time firmly reserved for them. Be playful. Remember what flattering names you used to call each other. Or how you have laughed for no reason, just because you were happy to be together. In the joint life more than anything, the danger is neglecting the jocularity and playfulness.

When people live a long time together, they say: "Hold on" as an adult. Or: "Not in front of the children!" But playful intimate relationships do not depend on age. During the game, intimate touching one another more than anything else strengthens relations between the partners. The gentle pat, the unexpected hug, can say: "I love to be with you" more convincingly than words.

- **Surprise each other.** If you do something unexpected for your partner, it shows that you have thought about him. The surprise says: "You were with me mentally even when we were not together."

  It is not necessary for this to be a great gift. A woman will remember such a surprise as: her husband got up in the early morning, bought her a rose, and served her breakfast.

- **Laugh together.** Many partners have laughed often together, but over time they laugh less and less. The joy of communication can be restored. A man tried to remember the jokes and the funny stories occured throughout the day to tell them at night to his wife. The woman hangs cartoons on the refrigerator. You can rent comedies to laugh together. The joke that both partners understand makes them closer.

  It is estimated that the partners who laugh at one joke, probably will live longer together. The same sense of humor

50

shows that they have the same life values.

- **Return the joy in your intimate relations.** This may very quickly become a habit faster than any other relations between the partners. Relations in this field are too little subject to change. Diversity gives excitement to the proximity between the pair.

  True proximity does not always begin in the bedroom. Touching and gentle banters mean hidden hints and increase pleasure by the actual closeness.

So a few years after one couple began a joint life, they found that taking a shower together is an excellent introduction to the proximity. Very often people concentrate on the sexual act itself and ignore the other resources that deliver joy.

For most women the hug and the presence of their partner may be more important than anything else. The joint life blossoms into rays of friendship and stability, but the waft of the new things and disengagement is also necessary not to fade away. The joy is important. To the happiest couples there is always a fun atmosphere.

# The Good Dialog

One of the most common situations in the lives of engaged couples occurs when the dialogue is lost between them. Even in families where husband and wife are married for years and know each other better than anyone else, a failure of understanding can occur just because they know their characters, but not their "internal" languages.

Imagine the following situation: a husband decides to surprise his wife and books a table in an exotic restaurant for a romantic dinner. He orders wine, everything seems perfect, but in the moment that they leave the restaurant she becomes extremely disgruntled and tortured by a terrible headache. Why did it happen like that? It's basic; his internal language does not match hers. He relies entirely on his eyes as a means of expression and perception and this defines him as "the observer personality"; she is operating under subconscious perceptions. These type of people have "the listener personality."

So, back to the romantic image. The restaurant—although very polite and pleasant—is full and extremely noisy. And despite the perfect view, their table is right next to the kitchen. This does not affect him, as he perceives with the eyes, but it bothers her in a way that even she cannot define. Quite often even we cannot realize our reactions in certain situations.

The idea of "internal" languages comes from a particular exercise in psychology called neurolinguistic programming. It summarizes the notion that some of us perceive the world according to what we see, others as what they hear, and others what they feel in a given situation. The problem is that these differences are invisible and unconscious. Like the wife in the restaurant, we rarely can understand why the differently designed people are not influenced by these situations the same way we are.

In love, these languages play a vital role. To have smooth romantic relationships, learn to read this internal language of your partner. The ability to lead your love relationship will grow only if you allow these features in the character and behavior of your partner to become clear to you. From there on it will be much easier for you to read the various states of your man and to avoid a significant number of conflicts. The three different types of people according to their internal orientation are:

- **The observer personality.** These women and men are interested mainly in how they look and are always dressed appropriately for every occasion—even if it is working in the garden. If you ask them a question that requires concentrated thinking, they'll look up, as if trying to visualize the answer. As a matter of fact, they do exactly that, and usually through the design of color images and pictures. This type of person usually reacts slowly as far as the expression of emotions. The best partner for them is another "supervising person," as they perceive mainly with their eyes. If a"listener" or "sensitive" person becomes their partner, there will not have continuous relations, because they always require more than the "observer person" can provide. Compromises are possible, but only if both partners are willing to make them—only then is a successful union possible.

- **The listener personality.** These personalities are generally good communicators. They love to talk and have the ability to read the mood of a person just by his timbre. They are sensitive to the sounds of the words and are often too analytical; they notice the fluctuations and prefer to call things as they see them rather than making hints. Before they answer a question, they will slowly slide their eyes left to right as if they are watching a tennis game, as they quickly think how to answer as if having an internal dialogue. The listener personality is a good partner of either of the other two types. Not to notice your new haircut is something usual. They are more interested in the internal world of a man, about how his mind works. They will listen devouringly how your day was and all your future plans. From them you can look for advice and you can know that they will be always there for you. To talk their language is as easy as saying "I hear what you say."

- **The sensitive personality.** This type of person is the most spiritless and always wrapped up in their own thoughts. They do not care about their external appearance. They love to eat, to rest, and are particularly loveable. Before they answer a certain question they will look down as if to consult with their internal presentiment and instincts. They are suitable partners for each type. Although they relatively occupy the final place on the scale of the demonstration of emotion, they are concerned with the mood of the person who is with them. They are grounded to provide a good education and to give a good example to their children and are always especially sympathetic.

As you can see, understanding the internal language of your partner can clarify many ambiguities in your relationship. Another time it could be as perfect, quiet, and harmonious, that it can even looks boring.

What is love? Chemistry that everybody is looking for.

# Get Under His Skin

*E*very woman has her own vision of how to flirt. More importantly, however, is the question: what are men impressed by?

- **Women must make the first step.** I do not mean that you should sit on his lap or send him a kiss just because it looks dazing. I talk about those hurried looks and smiles with which to show him that you are interested in him. He will take this as carte-blanche action and you will boost his confidence.
- **The expanded pupils are sexier.** There is a whole investigation on the subject that proves women with expanded pupils seem to be more attractive than those with shrunken pupils. Thinking about something nice, attractive, and loved also encourages pupils to widen. As I already said, the pupils are expanded when you are in love.
- **Light touching kindles the flame.** Along with earnestly expressive looks, another way of sending signals is touching. He will not know that in your head are developing some scenarios with his participation if you lightly touch him in every suitable moment. When you pass over in the club or when he is inclined to tell you a terribly interesting story, touching him on the hand or the back will show him that he is on the right path. Touching of intimate parts and slapping of the ass you can leave them for a few dates later.
- **Better to just smile than to be beautiful but pouty.** If you really want the man to notice you, approach, talk, and smile.

The smile brightens the face and all men like this. The pouty face and scornful glance will beat the man back.

A sense for humor is mainly for men. Unbelievable, but a fact. While women are dying for a man with a sense of humor, the reverse is not entirely true. The important thing is to laugh at his jests, but not for you to always make the jokes. Men consider it their own responsibility and privilege to make women laugh and if you take their role they will pull back. This does not mean to remain silent as a stump. Each witty word and well-spoken speech will put red dots in your column.

Of course, you can also make jokes but not as often as men and you must tell them at the right time. You should make up your face and prepare to smile as much as you can. After the efforts made to win him, now you must take care to keep him as long as possible. Two things keep one man: friendly relations out of bed and great sex in bed. And because the relations "out of bed" are so unpredictable, it is easier to give advice for the relations "in bed." The best thing is that you can almost never be wrong. The desire of men and women for sex is always dictated by some simple rules that were in force even in ancient times.

**The first way: not too much, not too little.** To give every time, to be available at any time, any place and in every way is very nice, but only if your relationship is stable and there's no need to prove to one another. But when you're at the beginning and neither you nor he is sure how your relationship will proceed, then it is better to keep the desire alive. This is when having balance between available and not is so important. Allow him to obey every time, but do not pull too long. Flirt with him every day as if you have not yet slept.

**The second way: boost his confidence.** Men need to feel significant, important, and unique. Never compare him with your ex-boyfriends. This is a way to lose him forever. Praise him for things that he does well, especially in bed. Even if it looks as a porn movie, a short whisper of "it's great" will make him try even more. However, never lie him. If there is something you do not like, something that does not deliver you pleasure, just tell him carefully how you feel. Do not forget to remind him of the things that he does great. Otherwise, he may decide that you are too "complicated" and seek a woman who can be satisfied more easily.

**The third way: promise him less, give him much.** The most awful thing that you can do to a man is to promise him that a naughty sex evening awaits, and then appear in a sweat suit and in front of the TV when he arrives home. Never do that, ever.

If you do the opposite, however—telling him that you are not in the mood, but then you appear in a lace nightgown—he will be the happiest man on earth. Always promise him less and surprise him with much. Incidentally, this advice can be applied not only in bed.

**The fourth way: keep the desire alive.** In order for good things to happen in the bed, there should be much experience and skill. No, this is not true. The fact is that when there is willingness and trust between partners, things almost always happen by themselves.

# Self-Confidence is an Aphrodisiac: Believe in Yourself

*C*onfidence is important for every aspect of your life, including love. Wondering what is common between the two things? The truth is that they are inextricably linked and always go hand in hand. Why is it important to be confident and to respect yourself in your love life? Let us look at two situations.

There is a girl who is charming and seems to be much liked by men. However, she is always smiling furtively, behaves politely, never emphasize her qualities, and never flirts. She always says "No—nonsense!" when somebody gives her a compliment and claims that she never succeeds with men.

There is another attractive girl who is communicating with confidence and does not feel bad when people are looking at her. She talks about successful and unsuccessful relationships and short flirts and is not too excited about what people will say about her because she knows that she is beautiful and smart. She dresses well, but her beauty comes more from the tone of the voice, manners, look...

I do not think that you doubt who is more liked and chased by the men. Now imagine that these girls are one girl and the vast difference between them is just a few months. She has become confident and feels good in her skin. She feels that she can have the man who she likes and does not bother to act to implement her wishes. She is confident in a positive result because she is sure that things will happen in the right way. Her point of view is, "I am sure that I like him and I am going to show him that I am interested in him. He will be mine!"

If for any reason things do not occur as planned, she will think that it would have been for the best. She believes in herself and is sure that she will find the man of her dreams who will respect and love her. She simply will not accept anything but the best for herself and would not be with a man who does not meet her desires and criteria. She respects herself and looks very proud to allow someone to refer to her with contempt. Even when they are in a relationship, men comply with her, stay with her because they respect her and want a woman like her to be with them. Those who are "dismissed" failed to respond to her wishes.

Now imagine that you are this girl. Confident, liked, and happy. A girl who can be with the man who deserves it. In love, there is no place for modest and fearful people. Believe in yourself and love yourself. Only by this way will others love you too!

You acquaint with him and he is wonderful...

You spend a lot of beautiful moments together, you taste the romance, feel the fragrance of love, and suddenly—he shows his dark side. Take a cold shower and quickly return to the land because you are a reasonable person who knows that love is not a question of devastating compromises. Do not demean yourself in the name of the love.

Here are the five golden rules with which you can check what is going on in his mind. If the games have toughen, take your pants, bags, and hat and raise up highly the shield of your female dignity. Do not waste your valuable time with someone who does not deserve it.

- **Golden Rule No. 1:** If he abuses you—whether in front of other people or privately—think very well how he will behave later after you have forgiven him this dirty word. Verbal insult is as damaging for this weak male creature as a physical violation. It can hurt to death that you will no longer see his big eyes, but believe me, it will quickly pass if you act boldly.
- **Golden Rule No. 2:** Do not try to be something that you are not. If someone does not like you, better let him find something that he will like. Never, never, never make compromises with the nature of a relationship. The pseudo-tolerance between your characters will soon say its heavy word and you will bump your head for that you have not realized it earlier.

- **Golden Rule No. 3:** If he does not stand for his word, then send him home. Confidence and security are the first, most important things in a relationship. Do not forget that.
- **Golden Rule No. 4:** If he does not stop spoiling his own world, do not turn into Mother Teresa. While trying to infuse sanity into someone's head or beginning to forsake yourself in order to help your "precious" man, then you better prepare to spoil your world. You can not be held liable for the entire universe.
- **Golden Rule No. 5:** The last rule is often ignored not only by females, but by lovers in general. If your guy does not respect your closest relations and talks badly about them (even trying to set you against them), do not just chalk it up to "expression of personal opinion."

The person who does not show respect for your family and closest people does not deserve even a drop of your tolerance. Listen to this advice and pay attention to the peculiarities in the behavior of the man next to you and you will prevent side effects such as broken heart, tormented mind, and shaken nerves.

Be strong, proud, and do not make any compromices for the destructive slops of another man until the day comes in which you find the guy that deserves your love.

# *Types of Men: Playboys*

*P*eople have become very greedy. All they want is everything and in big quantities. Our personal relations are no exception, where from the dream of love we have reached the cult of constantly changing partners. Everyone has the right to live as he likes. It is normal in life to have three, five, or seven partners, but if you cannot remember exactly how many people have passed through your bed, you probably have become a victim of the syndrome "sleeping with everybody just to increase your number." It is not a diagnosis but a lifestyle, which some people have chosen. Here are the types of such men:

- **The Collectors.** For them, the flirt is an art. They behave with every partner as if she is the only one, but only till the morning. Then they write down the name of their conquest in their little black notebook and continue to search for new women. The girl must meet certain requirements and a Collector would not make any compromises on that.
- **The Hunters.** The most important condition is not to come back home without a trophy. There is no criterion; the main rule for them is that the person who selects, he jerks off. The sad thing here is that in pursuit of quantity, the quality significantly declines.
- **Men with Complexes.** These people are constantly trying to prove how great they are—to themselves and to those who are around them. They are full of doubts and fears, the biggest being that they cannot keep a woman for too long. Therefore, they choose to insure themselves by seeking a short-term venture.

- **The Experimenters.** For them, every night is an opportunity to find new emotions, and each new partner is an unexplored territory. These people are quickly saturated with everything around them and can not stand uniformity, especially in love!

And there are those who just have fun and do not think about the sequels.

# Learn the Language of Men

*I*t often happens that when you say something like, "Collect your clothes," "Do not throw your socks on the floor," "Wash the dishes, please," and so on, it turns out that you do not speak the language of your partner. He just does not react. Men hate such requests so when his automatic reply is "OK," you should know that he has not heard you and will not fulfill what you requested.

Of course, sometimes men are very morose, but here the question is how to make him listen carefully to what you say. Even changing the tone and the approach does not ensure success. And sometimes it appears that he did not hear you at all, regardless of the topic. His brain blocks the access of information to prevent the creation of a tense situation. Then you are the one who has to do something. You just have to help him to listen carefully. There is one solution: learn to talk like a man. Here's how to do it:

- **Immediately start the main topic.** Imagine this situation: you have fought with the bitch from bookkeeping because once again she has messed with your salary, only because the sweet colleague from the first floor invited you and not her for a coffee. You want to retell this to your man.
- **Do not rush into specific details;** men are not interested in them. It is normal for him to switch off and continue to watch television. Start with the back to forward—according to the female logic.
- **If you believe your story has at least four parts, think again.** Perhaps your man will deem that it consists only of two, if not only one part. There is need to tell four or five

67

subject lines simultaneously or to specify spicy specifics about any "hero" in the incident. He will be so quickly bored that he will stop paying attention. For this you should learn to edit well everything that you want to tell him. Then you will be really heard.

Yes, even though you try to speak clearly and succinctly to your guy, there is no guarantee that tomorrow he will throw the trash on his way to work. The language of men, however, is not difficult, and there is a way to get him to listen carefully.

Your man won't be interested in gossip about your colleagues, for example, so keep these details for your girlfriends. Also, remember that most men do not understand anything from nuances in the voice, hints, or other indirect commmunication. It is important to be specific and accurate in order to avoid misunderstandings. He simply recognizes the words for "things" and the words for "action."

Do not play games like, "Guess what mood I am in today?" or, "I suppose that I am all right." Men cannot understand that behind these words lies something more. Men get everything literally and they do not analyze women.

When communicating with your favorite guy, always use the right names and words, or the "clever creatures" will never understand you. Men just express themselves literally and expect women to do the same. If he is still not interested in your personal life it will be better to think about somebody else. However, you are not a house maid, who is available at all times, right?

# The 21ˢᵗ Century: Women Take the First Step

*I*t was simply unacceptable a hundred years ago for a woman to confess her feelings to a man. Things are different now and to see a woman who takes the first step is not a rarity. But do men like to be courted by women?

Naturally, all the answers are "yes, I like that," but this is followed by a number of clarifications and explanations. Men love to be pursued, because it boosts their self-confidence. The female's attention makes them feel liked and desired. If your goal is simply to spend one the night with the chosen man, there is no problem with proceeding more directly to the question instead of waiting for him notice you.

A good compliment and an expressive look right into his eyes is sufficient to show him that you are not indifferent. Having added to this one and a more challenging dance, it is very likely that he will agree to send you to your home.

But if you want something more serious than a flirt for just a night with the chosen man then leave him the active role. Men are hunters by nature and the easy prey simply do not deliver pleasure. Also, men do not like overly aggressive women, especially they originally had more serious intentions for them.

Once you've taken his number and he has taken yours, do not start sending him messages about love at first sight or proposals for a meet. Save your dignity and wait for him to make the first step. If you have demonstrated clearly enough that you have feelings for him and he finds you far more than just a nice girl, then there are all the prerequisites to meet him at least one more time. Let him feel like he has won you and do not make him feel like you are ready to do everything yet on the first date.

Even if you do not succeed in catching his attention do not give up. The rules of this game are implemented gradually and you will soon meet someone who will like you as much as you do.

# What Men Do Not Like in Women's Behavior

**M**ost often women complain of their ever disgruntled men who frown or yell without any reason. But have you ever thought what men can not stand in women?

Here are some of the many elements of behavior that are good to avoid.

- Saying that you are fully prepared when you are about to go out at night and compel him to wait with a coat in his hand while you are still in underwear and polishing your nails.
- Standing in front of your wardrobe and saying with despair that you do not have anything to put on, and then frowning when he tells you that you are beautiful with each garment.
- Repeating indefinitely that you are fat. And if he says that is not true, oh, horror! "Are you blind?" But when he agrees that you have gained some weight, you instantly offend him by telling him that his pot is bigger.
- Frowning when he returns home, leading to the question, "What is wrong?" and then answering, "You know very well what is wrong." And if he truly says that he does not know, you insist that he remember.
- When he has bought a new sweater and is proud that he has made the right choice alone, and you to tell him that he has made a big mistake with the color, the size, the knit, the sleeves, the price, etc.
- Not noticing that he has come back home, even after he has

71

crashed the door, turned the radio up loud, and left the water running; but still you do not answer his questions about what you have been doing or what is there to eat, while you stare at the TV.

- When after one endless dinner with friends, he whispers to you: "Let's go home," and you to answer "Yes"—but still do not to get up from the chair and make him wait for hours.
- When he has warned you not to use his safety razor and you use it anyway, then say that there is no comparison between the gentle hairs on your legs and the rough hairs on his beard.
- Agreeing with his mother that he has really gained some weight and that he should start a diet while he thinks that he has a good shape and does not want to change it.
- Remembering in details all dates of your joint life even the most minor—such as the first time you bathed together in the sea—and then being offended if he does not come that day with flowers.
- Disturbing him while he is reading. Exactly then you want to read him something very interesting just for a minute and because he is pretending that he does not listen you start to read it again and he is forced to hear it with a downcast face.
- Speaking when he is making complex accounts, talking nonsense when he speaks about politics with friends, sitting on the edge of the bathtub and talking to him when he has requested privacy and quietness. And you still talk...
- Getting up at a restaurant to rummage in his plate over and over again. When he offers to order the same dish, you refuse because you wanted just to try a little from his.
- Asking him whether he loves you just when he falls asleep and insisting for his answer.
- Falling asleep in front of the TV and when you wake up, asking him what happened. If he answers that he will tell you later (not to miss the thread) you start to argue aloud that it would be better immediately to tell you what happened instead of losing time for other stories.
- Pretending that you are a saint. It was long ago when women had sex for the first time on their wedding night. There is no need to hide your past because women also have a right to

enjoy themselves. It is important to find out if your boyfriend is one of those who rejoice that their girlfriend has not sat at home before they met, or one who wants his girlfriend to be among the few who has not visited the garden of pleasures.

- Criticizing other women. It is almost impossible to hear a woman make a compliment to another woman without a huge dose of envy and hypocrisy behind it. You will come a step towards perfection if you confess that the woman who sits at the next table has beautiful hair. This will not make you less attractive.

- Being jealous. Gratuitous violence is the biggest enemy of any relationship. If you've already created trust in each other, ignore "good" friends who ask you, "Are you sure that he really drinks beer?" If you put the question directly in front of him, this will hurt him and will make him angry. Men do not like to feel held tight to the wall. Do not do this to the man you love.

- Needing continuous support and care. Most women want to continuously hear from their partner how special, unique, and loved they are because they do not feel safe in their own qualities. The irony is that these women before the start of the relationship were very independent and free. To avoid getting your boyfriend out of his skin, figure out as soon as possible that since he is with you, he finds you beautiful, smart, and good—and there is no need not repeat it momentarily.

- Talk incomprehensibly. A favorite "game" of women is to answer with "everything is all right" when it is apparent that the truth is elsewhere. Usually after this the woman tells him that he is very callous, slow-witted, and tactless not to notice that she has problems.

- Dear women, remember: when a man says that "everything is all right," they really think that. When they hear that from the mouth of their girlfriend, they accept that this is the truth and stop asking. It will be much easier if you have any problems just to tell him what they are. Men do not read minds.

- Rushing into their personal space. A woman who is trying to arrange the tools in the garage or the deranged disks around the computer is a nightmare for every man. You should get accustomed to the thought that men need privacy as women need a place in which to arrange all their cosmetic products. It is very simple. You would not like someone to change the places of your toilet milk and make-up, right?

- Being too emotional. Men cannot stand tearful women, whether the tears are for a film, a broken nail, or a bad haircut. Most of all, men do not like it when their tearful girlfriends seek from them solace. Men do not know how to calm tearful women. So if you want to get sympathy for something, do not search for it with tears because it will not work.

- Shopping too much. The ability of women to spend a whole day in the mall without experiencing thirst or hunger amazes all men. But their biggest nightmare is to be part of this shoping mania. Save him that. It's good to have common interests, but the shopping will not be one of them.

- Talking constantly. Most women like to talk constantly. If you do not stop them, they are able to speak a whole day. Men are also curious to know what happened to one of their friends, but they do not want to know all the details. Leave him sometimes alone with his own thoughts.

- Using sex as a weapon. To show superiority, some women are ready to attack at men's biggest weakness—sex. Leave alone the natural needs of the relations. You will not achieve much if you "hijack" him by this way.

Men love women. They like the way they look, walk, talk, and smell. Women also like men and both genders cannot live without each other. Maybe you think that you can live without a man but you mislead yourself, so it is better to learn well the things that men do not like in women's behavior and try not to do them.

# Sweet Ideas for a Romantic Date

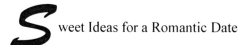weet Ideas for a Romantic Date

- Invite him to a private cocktail. The only people at the party will be you and your boyfriend. It is not so complicated. Use just a little imagination for the decorations and the cocktails. Small bites will fit beautifully in the situation, as will the soft light and the light music.
- Be crazy and young. Plan a meeting in a car or somewhere outside the city. Make sandwiches and if the weather allows, sit on the lid of the car together and have dinner while enjoying the beautiful view. And then...you know what...
- Have fun with fondue. Fondue is made with many French and melted cheeses. The delicacy in this case is that it is eaten with special grill whose end has a bit of bread. If you wonder where the romance is, the only way to eat fondue correctly is to include your tongue in action.
- Use foam and fragrance. Place of meeting? Your bathroom. The good part of this idea is that you do not need any clothes, which saves you a lot of headaches. Prepare chilled champagne and beautiful glasses. Also, get foam for the bath, candles, and massage oil. Choose only one flavor, to avoid an overly heavy atmosphere.
- Indulge your chocolate fantasies. The idea is similar to that

of the fondue, but includes lots and lots of chocolate. Pamper with more expensive chocolate temptations and remember to take liquid chocolate and milk to avoid becoming too sweet. There is no need for spoons.

# *How to Make Him Fall in Love with You*

*W*hat can you do to win him?

Everybody can claim that your hair is too long, wear short skirts, and spray your favorite perfume all over to win the attention of a certain man. But is that so bad?

No, of course—but only if it has an effect.

But in love as well as the consumption of biscuits, you should know the measure. You should not be misled; no matter how hard you're trying to win someone, remember that there are some unhappy (and uninclined) men who will never fall in love with you. So how far should a woman go to win the man of her dreams?

Here's the first rule: If you have any hesitation, if you feel awkward and even stupid about what you are doing in order to win him—just stop.

Second rule: There is no need to torture yourself without being sure that he will like you. But if you're happy with your long hair and short skirt, if the fragrance of your perfume makes you feel beautiful, exquisite, and sexy—why not to do it?

Let me be more specific:

- Should you talk to him?

    Yes, otherwise how would he know you are alive?
- Should you invite him on a date?

    Yes, all men feel great when a woman asks them for their phone number. He feels great to know that she is interested in him—and doesn't have to take the first step. Nowadays, men like the women to do that. And do you know something curious? The most successful relationships and marriages are made thanks to the first step made by the women.

Earlier in this book I advised you that if you want a serious relationship, wait to let the man to make the first step because men by nature are hunters. But nowadays things are different because most men are insecure and they have low self-confidence, so they are afraid of rejection. This situation has developed following women taking many male positions. Emancipated women made men lose part of their large confidence level. Imagine that the guy who you want likes you but is afraid to take the first step because he thinks that he could be rejected by you. Therefore, most of the men expect you to take the first step.

There are still hunters who want to fight for their loot, but most contemporary men are afraid of rejection by women. It is your choice what to do, but remember that whatever you decide to do, never regret your actions.

- Should you change your external appearance and style?

  Appraise whether to change your style and appearance by whether he wants you to do that. But if this change makes you feel oppressed, do not do it. Dress to feel good and beautiful.

- Should you pretend to be somebody that you are not?

  No! If you pretend to be someone you are not, he will fall in love with a spoofed image and not the real you. The game cannot continue forever.

- Should you cancel a meeting with a friend because of your partner?

  To leave a friend is an extremely serious offense. Moreover, your boyfriend will think that you are desperate and that you cannot breathe without him.

- Should you play hard to get?

  Sometimes the idea is not bad. Consider who is more interesting to you—the man who follows you everywhere, or the one who seems to like you but maintains uncertainty and expectation. If you are convinced that a man who is not interested in you would suddenly and desperately fall in love with you if you started to avoid him, throw a party and show him that you can have fun without him.

How should you engage the attention of a man? There is nothing more simple than being secure in yourself, mysterious, sincere, and fun.

- Put aside your own aggressiveness, even if it is caused by contact with him.
- Don't describe to him your life or affairs. That which makes a man desire you continuously is his own sense of uniqueness. He likes both surpises and mystery.
- Do not show yourself as self-centered.
- Always take part in his cares and share his expectations, because a man who feels that he is an object of interest is half won.
- Avoid doing "analysis" on him. Men do not like women who constantly judge them.
- Arm yourself with confidence; give yourself the look of a conqueror; flirt and be a carefully maintained woman, but without excess. Men like those who know their price.
- Be spontaneous in your imagination. It enhance your personal charm. The authenticity remains a very important trump card to be attractive.
- Try your best to make your gestures and movements look like a "cat"—sensitive and full of sensuality. It will be easier if you believe in your head that you are fascinating.
- If you have an occasion to dance with him, know that men recognize the sensuous woman by the way that she dances.
- If you see in his eyes a growing interest in you, remain calm and be careful not to show your interest in him too quickly.

Perky looks over the bar, cryptic smiles, and light squints with your eyelashes are a small part of women's armory to attack the opposite sex. However, sometimes the target is simply not responding. At other times, someone who you want only for a friend, decides that you have invited him into your bed. All this has a very logical explanation: much of women's sexual (non-verbal) signals are lost irretrievably in the minds of the men. They often do not understand the signs of the fair sex and confuse their reactions and the emotions that produced them.

Men often fail to distinguish between sexual interest demonstrated to them, friendliness, or complete rejection. They often confuse the amicable terms with the desire for a more intimate proximity and vice versa. There are men who are more experienced and correctly read the signals of the women. Besides, the fair sex has become more aggressive and clear in what they want from men.

Some women use business cards to expand business contacts. Others have them, but do not know how to use them. They are very small cards on which are written the most important things about you. But these business cards can also be used for much more personal goals. Imagine the following situation: You are in a bar. It is loud and dark there and your friends want to leave the bar. However, a very sexy guy has just come arrived and it is obvious from his and your eyes that there is an attraction between both of you.

While you wonder whether to stay in the bar, your friends carry you to the door and your fantasy evaporates into the air. With a sexy walk and without saying a word, you pass him facetiously your card. Then you immediately turn and leave the bar, careful not to stumble on the leg of a chair, and hope that the guy will soon call you.

Of course there are risks of such familiarizings. When you give your pasteboard you are giving your most important data—job, position, telephone, and e-mail—so do not distribute them as playing cards. You can do "party cards"—only with your name and telephone number or e-mail. Men would be very happy from such a performance and will call with pleasure. Be brave and prudent and act!

# Body Language: The Key to His Heart

Not every tremulous contact between man and woman leads to wild sex. If any sexual touching was prelude, consider how often and at what locations lovers would express their desires every single day. The yearning for physical closeness is not always dictated by sexual impulse. The holding of hands, hugging, massage, petting of hair, sitting in the lap of the partner—all these acts are caused by the longstanding desire for security and peace.

Learn not to enjoy only the sexual contact with your partner. This mode of communication will help you to harmonize and improve yourself and the sex.

- Arrange in advance a date and specify that its purpose is not sex, but simply a celebration of touching.
- At a convenient occasion share with one another where and how you would like to be touched.
- The light and gentle touch is the most tremulous, most relaxing, and most preferred. Try to be more creative when you stretch to caress him.
- Show one another where you prefer to be held during the kiss.
- Try to kiss your partner in the same way that you want him to kiss you. This is not criticism of the kiss, it is just a new feeling.
- Remember the goal: establishing a climate of emotional warmth, love, and affection, but no sex. If you're still unable

to resist the magic of purposeful touch, you can go to the end, but only if you both want it. Remember that touching and hygiene always go hand in hand. If the personal hygiene of one of you is lame, the pleasure of the touch will be lessened by half.

- Occasionally take a shower together. Contact with water and the body of your beloved will be a double peace. The back is a great zone for fondling with a massage. Furthermore, all people love to be massaged on the neck and around the waist.
- In the case that certain favors of your partner do not give you pleasure, tell him delicately about that and direct him how and where to nurse you. Never say: "Stop ...!" or something like that. Your behavior should predispose him.
- Communicate with warmth. A prerequisite for achieving satisfying contact is to be aware of your own and your partner's feelings. Express your love by caressing his face with your fingers. Do it even if you are spouses with twenty years' experience.
- Ensure that both of you have equal opportunities to give and receive equally. This principle applies to the "quantity" of the perfect touch. Caress him slowly, softly, and gently, and express verbally your admiration of his physical appearance. If either of you have a complex about any part of your body, for him such communication would not be so easy. Therefore help him realize that every part of his body is attractive to you. Most easily this is achieved by necking. Develop a positive attitude toward your own body.
- Learn to love him, regardless of the love handles, spare tires or short legs. Only if you learn to like yourself will you be able to enjoy full physical contact with your partner. Talk about something very intimate while caressing each other. During the night sleep as much as possible with fewer clothes. Nightgowns and pajamas should be more scarce, so you can touch without hindrance. Practice breathing together in rhythm as both lie turned on one hand: sleep with breasts pressed to the back of the other partner and with hand on his abdomen (to assess breathing and to follow his beat). Then change places and repeat the exercise. Try to go to bed at the same time and adjust your sleeping. All other options are

annoying and painful.

- Each night give yourselves fifteen to thirty minutes to lie hugging in the darkness before starting to dream. In this posture whisper innermost thoughts and small daily experiences. This is the time to tell your partner things that in other circumstances you would not dare to tell. In his embraces the insults and the disappointments of the day disappear. Create a good habit of making some kind of physical contact just before sleeping: for example, touching the arm or the leg of your partner. Hold hands more often. While you hold him try to use the "liaison" as a cable that is fueled by positive emotions. Sit down close to one another while watching television.

- It is not dangerous to be huddled in his lap, even while he is looking at a football match. According to statistics many couples spend their evenings in front of the TV. It would be a sin to waste this time without touching. Remember that the romance, the warmth in the relations, the sweet banters, the friendly kiss, and all aspects of touching are not only the privileges of teenage infatuation. Do not think that sex is the only way to remind your partner that you perceive him as a creature of the other sex. Therefore, touch each other more often.

# How to Maintain Your Position in Front of Him

*A*re you ready too often to do anything to please your partner? What do you get in return and what do you lose? Is it worth it to neglect yourself in order for your partner to be glad? There is an opinion that a woman's "no" means "yes." Men most often remember this rule when they encounter our unwillingness to give in to sex. Of course, they always prefer when women neglect their desires. And how does the woman feel?

It is long believed that women are whimsical and frivolous creatures with whom there is no need to comply, and until the late-Middle Ages the question of whether women have souls was still unclear. Do not think, however, that these thoughts from the past are not relevant to you. To the contrary, a large number of modern men quite frankly do not understand why their partner is not a nice dolly and is an independent woman with her own views and lifestyle.

Are times changing?

In the past it was simple and clear: the wife spent her life around her husband. She is that which he wants to see in her and with the help of the artistic gifts given by nature she often succeeds. Another question is, At what price?

Some handle it very easily, but for too many women it is quite severe, especially in the sensitive area of the matrimonial life—sex. For centuries, women kept their sex lives not as they wanted or needed, but as men desired.

Now, if you think something has changed, you are wrong. Our "friends" continue to abandon us, if we don't soon jump in their bed. We agree and do everything only not to lose their love. What we win is almost nothing.

It is true that the woman is able to change herself a thousand times—in the offices, in the tram, and in public. But there occurs a time when she ceases to be an actress—alone with her favorite person. In those minutes each wants to feel like she is his goddess. All roles except her own become unnecessary. But this moment of an absolute closeness is painful and distasteful for many women. How many representatives of the fair sex, with hand on their heart, can say that the sex with their partner is always satisfactory, that they never had to grit their teeth? It is true that in this delicate area, only the pros and some lucky ones can boast. The rest must endure.

During the sex act we rarely remove our mask desired by our partner, one of a passionate lover who is always and everywhere ready for sex, or a lady who doeos not even expect a call from him after the love night.

This is considered somewhat calm and steady—but how else? The most that a woman can do is to refuse some forms of the sex that are bad for her. The man, however, does not waiver in hoping to release her from her complexes. When accepting the foreign conditions in bedding, we rarely think why we do it. In the end, we not only do not receive any sexual pleasure, but also undergo severe stress. Many women forced unwillingly to satisfy the desires of their partners feel raped. Indeed, they rarely talk about it, preferring to suffer. But maybe they are not right...

How to combat inequality? According to psychologists, many women have an implanted feeling of guilt involving men, putting them in a sacrificial position where they do not even fight for equality. This is very convenient for the strong sex. The problem is not only of the long-standing male habit of not listening to the woman, but also the lack of respect for her. Indeed, we must confess—the compliance often identified with femininity is not always positive. Sometimes it is needed to refuse. Of course, you should also be able to step back. Only then can you assess the other side.

As a rule, equitable relations are established between strong personalities who feel well and do not only confirm themselves for someone's account. For harmonious couples, the question of leadership in sex almost does not exist. The sexual dialogue delivers more pleasure from the eternal struggle.

What to do when they force you? If you are not ready or do not want to accept everything that your partner proposes, you should offer something that you do like. Indeed, to do this, carefully use your female intuition and tact. Not all men like the initiative to come from the woman. The more active position will make the relations with your partner equal—you think and then offer and he may agree or refuse, but do not take offense. One more important thing: never repress even the smallest problems that occur in your relationship. Every woman dreams of a perfect relationship when the man and the woman form a union. However, the absolute transparency in relations between the two, despite the generally accepted concepts, can lead to misunderstanding and tension.

For years psychologists pointed out that to strengthen a relationship and to continue for a longer time, both partners have to speak for everything. Nowadays when the communication is the keyword for each relationship, these psychologists realize that sometimes the silence is more beneficial. It is clear that the whole truth should not always be shared and that 100-percent confidence sometimes means a real danger.

Intimacy is the sense that unites the couple. Unlike relationships in which the children play an important role in the family unity, unmarried couples need intimacy with which to connect them. The memories of proximity between the two should be kept green and they do not belong to the one or the other partner, but to the couple generally. It is uncertain, however, that sharing everything strengthens the intimacy—even the opposite is true. Intimacy and sharing are two different things. The stronger a couple is sexually, the more they express intimacy in recognition of the wishes and needs of the other.

In short, intimacy is a recognition of the personality of the human next to you. Each partner is entitled to retain part of his or her individuality. Moreover, this helps maintain a flame of desire. The obscurity is the main "ingredient" of the seduction. To share the moments of joy, happiness, or misery, to be available to him when he needs a shoulder on which to cry, while simultaneously with this you keep your individuality intact—this is the key to a real mature relationship.

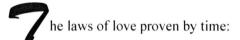

# The Laws of Love

*T*he laws of love proven by time:

- If you want to have him with the idea that you should change him you better not have him at all.
- If he tells you that he loves you more than sex, he does not mean exactly that.
- If he says that you are very special it means that he still loves you.
- If during sex he tells you that he loves you he is probably sincere. If after sex he tells you that he loves you he is probably lying. But if during breakfast he tells you that he loves you, he definitely means it.
- If he asks you: "How was it?" Control your impulse to ask: "How was what?"
- Two people never love each other equally. As the French say, there is one who kisses and the other who is just passing his cheek.
- The woman needs to be respected by her lover. Men do not need a respected wife—it is enough for them to like her.
- To have great sex you must feel completely free.
- Choose a man who is strong and pure but not a man who has nothing except money.
- It is a nightmare for a man when the woman is a whore in the kitchen, a cook in the living room, and a princess in the bed.
- Love is a risk.
- A man who resolutely refuses to use condoms does not

deserve to be slept with.

- The man can tell you that he wants you to love him. But actually he wants you to need him.
- The man often wakes up with an erection. But do not misread that the merit is yours.
- Men like lipstick lighter that the one that you like.
- Do not make a bad joke with yourself by forcing to accept him physically. If you really do not desire him at the beginning, most likely you will not accept him at all.
- Do not meet with a man with whom you would not want to have sex in the future.
- You should not wait until the bitter end.
- Do not present yourself as a manipulator. This irritates the men.
- You can be nowhere lonelier than in an unhappy and doomed relationship.
- There is no sense in marrying him if your relationship does not go.
- There is no sense in making a baby if your marriage is not running.
- Most women pretend. This also applies to you. Men also sometimes pretend.
- Better to tell a man that you are not attracted to him, rather than giving vain hopes.
- It is better to be loved and abandoned than never be loved. No matter that it will destroy you and will throw you into hell.
- It is healthier to be ribald than credulous.
- The foreplay should begin at least one week in advance.
- The road to indifference starts with love at first sight.
- Just because men do not talk about feelings, this does not mean that they are not experiencing them.
- Sex is a fence that you should jump over to find your own capacity for intimacy. Sometimes you can fall on a very thorny hedge.
- The bedroom is not a place for solid sarcasm.

# Things that Will Make Him Feel Happy with You

## Fashion Tips

**M**ost men do not understand fashion and rarely are willing to experiment with their clothes. They create a certain style at the age of seventeen or eighteen and there is not anything to convince them that ten years on is not appropriate to go with a shirt and sneakers to formal dinners.

The role of women in this case is to tactfully explain to their beloved the basic fashion rules. Men are happy when they feel that their partner cares about their appearance. In no case, however, should you speak as his mother. Something like, "I am trying to help you" is much more effective than "I will be ashamed to go into the streets with you if you are dressed like that."

## Compliments

Compliments for a man are the looks and the touching. He is rarely as impressed by words as women are, although he is very happy when you tell him how sexy he looks with a suit. But if he "catches" you looking at him with pleasure from head to toe he will feel really special.

**Dress sexily** (but not only in bed).

Remember that your partner considers you the sexiest woman on the planet. If it were not so, you would not be together. Show him a little more flesh and not just in bed. Most men love to see that their girlfriend attracts the looks of other males. However, the border is fine; do not behave provocatively with everyone else, but only and entirely with your partner. When you are at home, wear something comfortable but sexy. This will keep your emotional relations pleasantly warm.

## A happy partner

Men have two concerns in the world: They don't want to lose their hair too early and they don't want to lose their sense of humor. Nothing makes a man more happy than to be able to make the woman of his dreams laugh. And since women also find attractive those men who manage to make them laugh, the task is not so difficult. Men are very rarely willing to say what they really like, especially when it relates to the daily relations with their girlfriend. To hear a woman saying "I want to be embraced more often" is normal, but a man will never say it. Therefore, here are a few small gestures that men love but never dare to ask for.

**Small surprises.** Show your lover that you think about him even when you're not together. Get him something he has mentioned that he would like to have. Just do not buy him fashionable shirts that you want him to wear. Some men get mad over this. And as I said earlier, do not buy him presents if you are at the beginning of the relationship. You should be together for a little longer to give him surprises such as gifts.

Show him information about his favorite team or record a movie he missed because he was busy working, etc.

**Unexpected hugs.** Kissing and all kind of touching are required, especially in moments when you see that your man is tense. Show him that you sympathize with him by touching him on the hand; this will encourage him.

Palm his back while passing behind his chair, it is guaranteed that a shiver will pass through his whole body and he will feel really loved.

**Increase his confidence.** Men need to feel like "the man" in the house. Most of them even manage to be, which is calming in terms that do not require women to do everything by themselves. Do not belittle anything that he has done/repaired/bought for home. He will feel really valuable.

**Personal time.** A typical situation: You both come home after work, you tell him how your day was, while he is surfing the Internet or through the television channels, and he answers you with gibberish. At this time in the woman's head begin to rotate issues related to the peculiarities of his character and the power of love and whether he is the right choice. There is no sense worrying over these things because the truth is very simple. Men can much better than women "exclude" themselves after a hard day. They want to have a rest and not think about anything. Let him have these moments of peace from which he needs as you need from a hot bath after work.

# 20 Things that Men Find Irresistible

*E*ach woman asks the logical question: "What do men like?" but there is hardly a woman who knows the exact answer. Men like women who:

- Know how to seduce and understand jokes.
- Know that men are not actually from Mars, nor women from Venus.
- Wear the T-shirts and the boxers of their partner.
- Kiss with imagination.
- Like the quality dispute.
- Watch or participate in sports competitions often.
- Gladly take a leading role in bed.
- Behave charmingly with their mothers.
- Can bind their hair just using a pencil.
- Look both smart and sexy (for example, they do crosswords dressed in sexy pajamas).
- Can elegantly suggest what present they want without converting the buying for an obligation.
- Are independent in spirit but do not make the man feel unnecessary.
- Know the difference between flirtation and friendliness.
- Can eat a huge portion of steak and chips without discomfort and then order a dessert.
- Nap next to their dear man.

- Send flowers.
- Know what the man wants from them.
- Know what a man likes to do.
- Know that men do not like sloppy women.
- Know their price and have dignity.

# The Kisses that Men Desire

Sex without kissing would only be a serious physical exercise. A candle-lit dinner without kissing would be only eating. The kiss is the easiest way to awaken a sexual desire with someone. If you kiss each day for thirty seconds, it will improve your sex life two times over. During a kiss, even if it is a short good-bye kiss, hormones are separating that improve the mood, unlock the desire for closeness, and act as starter of sexual hormones. Thanks to the kiss you can get your man to think about you all day. If in the morning and at the end of your last meeting you kiss him, there's no way to quickly get out of his head.

By the way, as you already read, kissing with imagination is one of the things that men find irresistible. Kissing on a tender place—ears, neck, back, palms of hands, or the fold of the bone—may make the most tired man want some necking. However, it is important to know about kissing before you want to have sex. Kiss is the legitimate way to express your love in a public place. You cannot have sex with your partner in the station. Since the kiss is the traditional home of sex it is believed that a hot kiss in the cab or in the restaurant will crucify the flame irresistibly.

The passionate kiss approaches the speed of the orgasm with the speed of light. And to kiss properly, there are some absolutely essential things that you must comply with in order to make the moment magical.

- **Soft lips.** Balms are obligatory even for men. It is terrible to kiss with cracked lips. It is not effeminate to apply balm and even most women are happy when they see a man who takes care of himself.
- **Fresh breath.** Avoid heavily flavored food and those that swell your stomach when you go on a date. Use a breath

freshener for your mouth; chewing gums and all that will make your breath fresh and pleasant.

- **Imagination.** As with sex positions, kissing must have diversity. The tongue and the lips are sufficiently flexible to be able to experiment with them. The only inconvenience is that at this moment your mouth is busy and you cannot tell whether you like something or not, but a light retraction will show your partner that this is not the most beautiful kiss.

# How Not to Scare Your New Boyfriend

here are some things that you should not tell your new boyfriend. They become "authorized" when you're together for at least half a year. With every new boyfriend women tend to think of marriage and children right on the second week. In this of course there is nothing wrong, because the biological role of the woman is unique; because she desires to continue the family, it is normal to accept every man in her life as a potential father.

As for men, they prefer to enjoy such a relationship as it is now, especially in the early relations. Men make joint plans for the future much more difficult and very rarely talk about them. For them the questions of women such as, "Do you love me?" "Is she more beautiful than me?" and others are very irritating because of the fact that he is with you—that alone means that he prefers you to the other women. Couples often split because the woman has sped up plans for which the man is not yet ready.

## Do not tell him that you love him. Not yet!

Many people confuse the falling in love with love, and are willing to say the two words only because they have spent the night or a romantic weekend with their new boyfriend. If you hurry with "I love you," it is very likely your partner will pull back from you because he will feel pressed to answer with the same and will still not be ready for that. Over the time, you will both get to the revelation that the feelings you have are more than a momentary flame.

**Do not tell him that you cheated on your ex-boyfriend!**

Even if your ex-boyfriend was a badass, a liar, and deceiver, adultery is not the most valiant way to show someone that he is not worthy. Furthermore, people say "someone who cheated once will do it again," so hold your tongue behind the teeth of the details about your previous relationships.

**Take your time to meet him with your parents!**

Nor invite him too soon to the wedding of your cousin. The presentation to the family is a sign that you both have serious intentions to one another. It is not said that you are going to marry, but acquainting him with your parents is a serious demonstration of your relationship. When you're together for a month or two it is better both of you meet your own parents, regardless of how much your mother insists to see him (his mother is also curious, but men somehow are able to divert the desires of their mothers). As for marriage, or any other family event, the logic is the same as with getting to know the parents. If you so much want to "show" him, go out with your friends and not with all the aunts and uncles who will begin questioning him about everything from the time when he was born. Enjoy the moment and time will show whether your relationship will become serious.

# *How to Avoid the Selfish Person Who is Not Able to Love*

*L*et's accept that you are one of the lucky people who has found "the man of your dreams." The miracle has happened after a series of unsuccessful relationships with dramatic separations. Even if they were not so many, you still feel at least temporary satisfaction. Then the initial euphoria of falling in love goes away and you start to ask the inevitable question, "Does he love me?" If you trust only the expression of the male sentiment then the chance to answer this question tends to zero.

The happiness is experiencing easy. But if more and more often you feel that he does not love you, the question is, Why?

There are always at least two options. One is that the reason is your own fault: the gentle, easy, and kind woman with whom he has fallen in love has become a hysterical and hardly bearable brawler. It is far more likely that he is just selfish. How to reveal him? Add a little eye to your intuition and you are ready!

- **He never says that he loves you.** Well, there is no need to repeat it constantly, but not to say it never, or mechanical "me toos" in your expressions of love is insufficient. Impulsive bursts during orgasm are not very convincing. Maybe not by chance he neglects to say the magical words "I love you!" and his feelings have really cooled off.
- **He hides you from his friends.** You hardly desire to attend

all-male gatherings. And it would be stupid to impose your company against his will. But maybe he ignores you utterly purposefully. This does not necessarily mean that there is something or someone to hide, but obviously he does not want to be with you everywhere. Or he does not like to "share" his personal friendships with you, which is a pure form of egoism.

- **He makes a big brawl if you are late.** Nobody has a crush on waiting, especially if you are late too often. If you are not such a sinner and you are together for a long time, it is not normal for your partner to make a drama of a several-minute delay. The acceptance of some of your weaknesseses is almost mandatory proof of love. Of course, unless you get a hog.

- **He is annoyed by success in your career.** Actually, he does not mind participating equally in the family budget even if your contribution is bigger. But the glory of the ruler at home he is guarding cautiously. So do not wonder if while you share your success in work, he stares at you blankly. It is probably because of very selfish reasons.

- **He throws up his hands at the smallest problems.** We all dream for family happiness, but reality is something quite different. And while we war with many trials that life presents us, we need a strong male support. But when the ego of your partner is too big, there is no way not to go into mental collapse in tense situations.

- **He leaves the care of the children entirely to you.** Childcare is a priority of the mother. That nobody disputes. However, the role of the father in children's education is fundamental. Maybe he tells you that the making of money occupies his whole time but if he really wants it he could combine both functions successfully. Naturally, if he is not too big a hog.

But what to do! The male ego is a bubble full of crushed female confidence. Every bubble is doomed to crack, but whether it is worth waiting? Use a pin! After that, quickly start the search for a man who will truly loves you.

Experience and years teach us to recognize the different types of men. Perhaps even when you see a man you put him in a certain category, saying something like: "This is a man for one night" or, "This is an easy prey and will quickly fall in love with me," "He is gooey ," "This is the man that I want and I want to make him fall in love with me," etc.

It is difficult to learn to recognize a man who is reliable and who would respond to your wishes. That is why women are constantly left with broken hearts and deceived expectations. The reason is that men easily mislead women who have crushes on them. And sometimes the women themselves are left to be fouled in the networks simply because they like it or idealize him.

Women are very different and each is seeking an exact type of man. In every life stage she needs a good relationship with the right man for her. The best thing in life is to meet the real man at the age of eighteen, twenty, twenty-five or thirty, and who will be with her until the end of her life. When you are eighteen years old you want something crazy, different, and not too serious. When you pass twenty-five years you look for the man of your dreams with whom to have children and to create home. At a later stage you already look for warmth, love, harmony... How nice would it be to live all those moments from start to finish with the one you love. Sometimes the heart does not hear the laws and you may fall crazy in love at the age of fifty, if so far you haven't found the right man. The problems come when you are confused in the assessment and when you have a crush on a man who brings you only suffering and dissatisfaction.

What are the main types of men for which should have a mind?

The one who quickly falls in love. You meet him and after one week he claims that he loves you. In the movies it is very romantic, but in life it is too unrealistic. If he has kindled quickly he could also quickly become bored with you. Only the smartest moves of a woman may retain his interest for longer, but this is not a guarantee. If you feel that his feelings fall from the sky and are not a result of the relations, you better keep your heart at a distance in order for it not to be broken.

Only time will tell whether this is really love or a momentary passion. But sometimes—romantic as it may sound—there really is love at first sight.

- The selfish guy. He thinks first for himself and then for the woman. Even if he starts to love you, it will be in his selfish way and if you are a girl with big heart you will often feel hurt. You want to go to the movies, and he says: "I do not want to go to the cinema. I prefer to do something else," and he will even not think that he can do it for you. If the case is serious, a change in his behavior will not occur. There are cases when the love changes the people but to the hardened selfish person it often goes the opposite direction—it changes the meaning of love.

- The eternal playboy. They have a neat pattern of behavior and sometimes are so limited that they flirt with every girl without changing repertoire. There is however a more advanced type of man who would take down the stars for a woman. Usually the "eternal playboy" looks very good and this facilitates his success. The symptom, which will be easy to recognize, is the lack of real interest—he will not listen you carefully when you talk to him and will not remember your previous conversations. For him it is not important who you are; it is important that you are beautiful and that he has a chance to sleep with such an attractive woman.

- The mismatch may not be a bad person but may just not be the right one for you. For example: You want to become a writer and you find the Russian literature unique, but he even has not heard of Dostoevski and considers writing a waste of time. Or: You seek the biggest love and hope that you will find it in his face but he does not believe in love and says that he will never fall in love and that mutual interest is more important. The differences in the values are almost insurmountable and similar relationships, in most cases, are doomed to failure. When the passion is kindled you can not notice how much you are different. Even if your man is from the "dangerous" type it is not a guarantee that it will not work between you.

The important thing is to be happy with the man next to you. The compromises that you do make should not make you feel incomplete and inhibited. And yet—there are men who should be avoided. You should determine who are the ones who should not be near you. No man is perfect. But some are less perfect than others.

Therefore, especially avoid:

- The married man. He will never be the man of your life. At least because the husband has the life of another woman—his wife.

- The divorced man. Especially several times. He claims that it was not his fault, that the first woman was stupid; the second, unfaithful; the third, hysterical, etc. And what will you be?
- The playboy. More than a thousand conquests and no marriage! Even if he repeats that it will be different with you, beware.
- The man-child. He lives with his mother. But you have your own mother and prefer to be the first in his life.
- The constant visitor to the psychoanalyst. He sprawls on the psychoanalyst's couch twice a week, and for many years. If so, will it be the same on the couch in your house?

# *He Loses Interest? Do Not Let This Happen!*

*D*o you wonder why he lost interest a little after he was taking down stars for you and he swore in the eternal truth?

There are several reasons.

The shiver of the hunter: You have spent a perfect night with someone, in which you shared so many things with each other—even hugged a little, and then: he does not call anymore.

Or you are together for several weeks. He is nice, polite, wonderful, while at a beautiful moment he becomes as cold as a rock.

All this is due to the aspiration and desire of men to fish. Some call it hunting, others—fishing. Skillfully they place the bait and they collect it, but ultimately the objective is the same: to have won a trophy.

Men do not only think about sex and are not absolutely insensitive. No, they just want more quickly to change "the situation." Nothing personal, this is hunting.

Alternatively, he has dumped you simply because he is afraid. Afraid that you may be the last, and he still does not feel ready to be bound forever.

There are many men who change their girlfriends because they want to recapture the first moments of any relationship, when everything is passion, understanding, and not very serious.

Do not give all ... immediately. The way to keep a man is too submit moderately the data about yourself. When in love every man tends to forget the whole world to sink into his new relationship. "Sinking," however, can drown the relationship because of overly strong emotions and feelings that have quickly exhausted.

Retain your autonomy. Do not be fast with joint plans ("we") and do not forget your friends. And even if the feeling is terrific, do not quite give over to it completely, so as not to disappoint strongly when it appears that you are not the woman of his life.

# The Male Ego and Why You Should Watch It

*I*n one film it was told: "If you pat man on his intimate place he will be yours for the evening. If you fondle his ego he will be yours for the whole life."

How much truth there is in these words.

Women must seriously observe the ego of their partner, because if they hurt him, problems may appear. But if you treat him correctly, the man will feel wonderful in your company.

For many men, dignity and a good image stand above all. They want to feel strong, sexy, and influential, good things that women also enjoy them but do not always get them from their partners. The male ego claims to be so strong and comprehensive and at the same time it is more fragile than the most wounded female soul. Most often men are affected by topics related to sexuality, financial capacity, endurance of character, and their professional capabilities. There is hardly any more embarrassing thing than telling a man that he is totally awful in the bed and that you have not experienced any sexual pleasure from your experiences with him. Or that he is the worst lover that you have had. And also that he has a strange little penis. Each man will feel terribly humiliated and will not want to see you anymore. The hurt ego of a man is a sure way to lose him forever. Men have a very difficult time being mocked, especially if it happens in front of their friends or in a public place. That's a way to be sure that he will remember it a very long time.

Women are used to being very careful about men's ego. But have you ever thought about why it is so? Why do most men literally suffer from their ego? At the core of the problem we can see the complexes of

109

men. Or otherwise, the higher his ego, the more complexes he has.

Men who hide essentially behind high claims and continually demonstrate hurt ego most likely suffer from a number of complexes and are highly uncertain of themselves. That is why men with big egos often humiliate their girlfriends and make them feel bad with offensive lines and rude comments. They want to shine in front of the woman, to feel more forward in every aspect of life—to have a better profession, to make more money, and to be stronger and smarter.

When a man fails to notice that superiority to the woman who is with him, he feels his ego has diminished and does everything possible to take a dominant position. It often happens that couples are separated because the woman is better in all qualities and the man cannot accept it and begins to create problems in their relationship. The successful and decent men who can offer much to a woman usually do not suffer from ego stings as much. Some men can be insulted so much by a harmless joke that you may think that you are communicating with a child. The confident men have the ability to understand the jokes and deal with female discontent. For others, it is easier to pout instead of considering whether the issue is caused by them.

Unfortunately, there are many couples in which the woman is always careful with what she says so as not to hurt the ego of her man. She makes fewer remarks and boosts his confidence. Indeed, the male ego is a valuable thing, but only in measured quantities. Every man has it, and we must respect it. However, if the ego starts to dominate in your relations and you start to care more about his image in his eyes than in yours, it is high time to leave him. His ego should not harm your relationship. The male ego should be a warm part of your strong man, which should make you smile.

# The Relations and Several Truths about Them

The relations between couples will never be easy, because when it comes to love, passion, and emotion, things are very complex. There are a few truths that you must follow in all your relations in order to clarify the relationship and to have less pain if it is time for separation.

- **Clarify what you feel and what you say.** Women often think that early in the relationship they should do everything in order to be liked by their partner and are aiming to please him at a maximum. It is better to be yourself in order not to give the wrong idea about yourself. True love is what occurs naturally and it happens when the partner accepts the real you.
- **Realism.** If love has met you with someone who is married and has obstacles to the "normal course" of the relationship, do not deceive yourself. You can stay friends, even for life, but very rarely are the obstacles overcome to let your love blossom. Do not allow them to deceive you with their stories, especially when you do not see action from him for months. You will need many forces in order to remove him from your life, but it's better to cry a river than suffer all life.
- **Intuition.** Listen to your inner voice. He cannot mislead you. That special feeling in your stomach is not influenced by friends, from prejudice, or by anything else.
- **The wonderful prince.** Do not wait for him because he does not exist. There are many wonderful people. Beauty is not always on the outside of a man. Beauty can be hidden in his

111

heart and soul.

- **Avoid overinterpretation.** If a man tells you "I am not ready to have a serious relationship," this does not just mean that he is afraid and that in time he will get used with it. It really means that he is not ready for a relationship at all. The best you can do is to separate as friends.
- **Communication.** It is normal for two persons to discuss their feelings, expectations, and preferences. The trust between two persons is constructed with every word and every conversation. If you cannot share your dreams with him, there is no need to be together.
- **Conflicts.** If you cannot say out loud what you do not like because you are afraid that something "horrible" will happen, know that your relationship won't last long. Once it appears that small daily problems can destroy your relationship, there is no sense in investing time and emotions in the relationship with someone who will "hold" for the smallest problems and will dump you for them.

# The Art of Being Happy Together

*T*he life of the couple in love does not always look like a lake on a summer day. The ability to maintain intimacy, mutual attraction, and respect—these are the secrets of happy coexistence. But remember that in love nothing lasts. Even after ten, twenty, or thirty years you cannot be sure that your relationship will be always stable.

The preservation of feelings is a living battle that requires constant attention. Listen to the wishes of your partner and try to understand how both of you change during the years. Learn to make compromises and above all—be aware of the direction in which your relationship develops. It all takes time, energy, and optimism. And being willing to live!

So perfect stories end with failure because our ideal of perfect relationships is very high. Usually we want to have everything: love, good sex, freedom, and opportunity for success. We live in a society which as a rule requires personal realization. A love life, on the contrary, is based on the condition that we leave the ego in the background. This does not mean you have to give up on ambitions and desires, but rather accept that life changes when you live with someone. Accept the weaknesses of you partner, and the inevitable small failures in the joint life. The happiness of both of you depends on a certain attitude and behavior that is cultivated and educated. Here are some tips to find yourself in the narrow area of the couple.

Build harmonious relations. To successfully mix the cocktail called life, you should put in dialog, listening, patience, respect, and dignity. "We hardly talk," "There is nothing we can talk about"—these are the most repeated reproaches between the partners.

He is immersed in silence and accepts all the reproaches before shaking the door behind him. You are tireless with efforts to take out one word from your dumb interlocutor and you often exceed all levels of good upbringing. Unfortunately, there is no single cure for this classic case. If you always remember that men have more difficulty speaking and their dictionary is worse than that of women, you will begin to pay greater attention to body language and gestures.

Resolve the conflicts. Learn to decipher the reactions of your partner, to read between the lines rather than to continually gripe and make petty comments. As you carefully watch his behavior you will learn much and will not be angry; you will understand what delivers him pleasure, what hurts him and makes him mad, and when it is not time to start a conversation.

The fact that a couple is quarreling does not mean that it is going badly. Scandals are hard to avoid when both are with hot blood. Delays, unexpected costs, inadequate behavior to the children: the tone of the voice sometimes rises for very minor things. It is difficult to keep self-control, especially after a hard day. Having the ability to control the conflicts is more important. Simple rules: destroy the ferocity of the scandal with a calm tone; give priority to the mind, not to the emotion; let your partner speak and listen to him carefully. The dissent should cause a search for a solution.

Avoid the traps of jealousy. Jealousy is normal. It is neither an ugly nor shameful feeling, but it should be in moderate doses and should be controlled. The puncture in the heart when your boyfriend is talking with a beautiful woman is understandable. But do not be aggressive; the espionage of your family becomes a threat to its existence. Men suffer too much from the maniac invasion of their girlfriends and wives in their personal space—whether it's fumbling in his pockets, or browsing in the phone book. It is a dangerous game in which jealousy plays a destructive role and completely rejects dialogue, especially when fears of cheating are unfounded.

Should we say everything? The desire for full transparency in relations is rarely healthy. The relationship can be destroyed by the confession of an affair, but in this case it is usually found that one partner uses the confessions as a means of settling accounts. Indeed, excluding systematic lies, sometimes it is better to shut up, unless you want to challenge a crisis in the relations.

Beware of conflict arising from your partner's family. Say you cannot stand his sister (mother or brother) or his best friend. He certainly knows that. You can even tell him that calmly. But when he talks on the phone with the person who you cannot stand, do not make bad comments and do not be angry that he continues to keep in touch with them. These repeated scenes seem harmless, but actually they deeply hurt the attacked one and helps sow the seeds of discord, which often occurs later. Better make a compromise and allow your partner to remain loyal and faithful to the members of his family. Manage to stand aside and do not interfere.

Keep your freedom. The future of a couple depends on the ability of both to continue to live their own lives without being fully dependent on one another. Some women do not dare to go to the movies without their boyfriends. They are not shy or limited, they have got work and have their own environment. Indeed, sometimes it is difficult to imagine, especially at the beginning of the relationship, that the other may feel pleasure from something which he does not share with you. And this is completely normal.

Everyone should have an independent social life to bring him satisfaction, because having one indirectly enriches and strengthens the relations.

Greet news of a baby calmly. The emergence of the first child in the family is a serious obstacle which the young must overcome together. Efforts are needed by both to cope with their new roles without violating their previous harmony. When the baby is born, everyone should maintain their own identity, while at the same time helping the new family of three. The preservation of intimacy is very important. Do not leave the baby in your room long to avoid harming your sexual relations.

Be approved of. Acceptance of the couple includes being welcomed by everybody. The relationship must be recognized by colleagues, family, and friends. This is sometimes complicated, especially if a partner has a great difference in age, social status, education, or repeated marriages. Difficulties accompanying recognition from others can lead to serious problems in the relations between the partners. The main thing in this case is to assert their love and to desire for a joint life.

# *How to Keep a Man Forever*

**T**oday, as permanent marriages have become a rarity, men prefer to be pulled out rather than accept responsibility, and women more often become like lonely seafarers. What to do to keep him forever? "The only victory over love is flight," Napoleon said. Today women continue to use this formula. People often say: "I do not want to be tied." There is not a woman who at least once in her life has not faced a similar and not very pleasant answer.

Men think that every woman is looking for marriage and the fear of a wedding ring hangs over their heads like a sword, even after the first night spent together. The children of today's consumer, throwaway society face major difficulties in establishing a stable relationship. However, all singles know some "real" couples—married or not—who make them jive with their welfare.

Here are some tips taken from those women who know the art of detaining a man.

Let's take for example a type of woman who has a remarkable talent to lead a man into her house together with his suitcase. Of course, she has had other men who have tried her kitchen, have hung their clothes in her wardrobe, and who have kept their toothbrush in the bathroom cupboard. They have held for some time, then they have separated, but everything has always passed easily and safely.

What's the secret?

The key is the ability to fully adapt to the newcomer. As such, a woman held primarily to be loved, she is ready to sacrifice all to reach her goal. Her tactics are confined primarily to complete faith in her intuition and a healthy instinct. This woman can immediately understand his tastes and preferences. If he likes weak and defenseless creatures, she immediately becomes a timid woman who needs protection. If he has a weakness for independent women, she organizes herself and for more authenticity often goes alone, even if it costs her a few days spent in the four walls of a hotel room.

She is like a real chameleon whose art consists of the ability to change its colors without even thinking about it.

What does the independent woman do?

At the beginning of the relationship she primarily behaves indifferently. She meets him accidentally in the coffee shop or on the street. Actually, she organizes a spy organization that monitors every gesture and movement of the man that she wants. When they do not see each other for a few days, she is careful not to ask him what he has done during this time. Even when she has spent a whole week next to the phone and he hasn't called even once, she remains calm and does not say anything.

This woman does not have fancy thoughts and never has illusions. She does not go to the new relationship or marriage with ideas about a pre-established ideal man—friend or husband. This is one of women's oldest tricks. It seems that a sober and realistic view on life is one of the most important conditions for creating a stable relationship or a stable marriage.

But even if the relationship is serious and consolidated, this behavior is appropriate. It requires above all compliance and knowledge of nerves—a key moment in the life of a couple. Any small "sins" inherent in every person should be dealt with philosophically. The realistic woman says in such moments: "What does the toothpaste have in common with the building of my marriage?" She knows how to get rid of her habits accumulated over the time she has been her own master.

This type of woman observes one golden rule. She respects her own independence. She never shows that she needs the guy that she wants, even if she has waited for him as a messiah. Instead of throwing her hands around his neck when he returns after a long absence, she leaves time to show how much she cares for him. Men are afraid of women who create scenes when they are late; they are afraid when women ask too many questions and are suspicious. Most of them prefer the independent behavior of the women who love them, but can deal great without them. They do not like much those who complain that they are lonely and unhappy, because they believe that once a person lives alone and is not happy, he will be the same in the joint life.

It should not be believed that maintaining independence is a tactic for bait. It is a lifestyle, which plays a major role in the long life of the couple. The full mental merger is dangerous and quite often damages. Everyone should have his own secret garden.

To be independent, you should be wary. To live so as to leave enough time for the other requires major acrobatics. You need to find a balance between autonomy and joint life, because if one depends too much on the other, inevitably over time it will give way. In short, the life of a couple requires some effort. Especially in the beginning when the relationship is still fragile, you should think of countless small wiles and pleasures that carry joy in the joint life.

Now comes the order of the organized woman, who in no case is walking all day in a dressing gown. She ensures nice atmosphere in the house, invites guests, and makes sure boredom does not come between them. Boredom is most hostile element in the lives of two people. And men do not like boring women. She takes care of the development of the couple, analyzes, and observes.

The family life is like a ship at the sea, and quite often women are those who have a psychological attitude and ability to manage it. Many people today do not see the joint life as a connection for the entire life. In order for a couple to be successful, they should earn it. Good reason to redouble the attention. With the passing of the years, the life of two people enriches, but to avoid being overrun by the daily gray life, each of them must be rigorous. It is not bad to maintain a gastronomic flame in a joint life. This is the true symbol of home—comfortable and cozy.

Here are some basic errors that you must avoid committing: You should avoid the men who lose and who have not yet emerged from adolescence. Remember that these types of men never change. Others who really are not "Supermen" may be persuaded to start a joint life. They may be afraid but they will try. Love and faithfulness are fundamental values. Time, habits, and crisis put the partners on trial.

How do you keep the love of a man? Here are some tips that many women know, yet still often forget:

- When in front of him, avoid walking around negligee, not dressed, with mule, with the apron that has a spot from the sauce that you prepared for dinner, with a mask of oily cream on your face, with grimy hair, etc.
- If he likes you sexier, do not hesitate to change the style of your wardrobe. You can retain your style but add something

that he likes. Or when you go out together give him the pleasure of seeing you dressed as he imagines you. Surprise him!

- Get control over the art of the surprise! Break the routine of the daily life. Plan a holiday for him. Surprise him with new unknown nice things. If you go home together at night, leave the work problems for the job. If you do not work and take care of the family, surprise him with something unexpected at home. Men are always grateful of spontaneous affection. In most cases men do not clearly show their feelings but every woman can see when her man is satisfied.

- Do not forget about your pleasures. Love is a shared experience. Concentrate on your own sexual desires in order to be fully satisfied. The ambition and the efforts to satisfy your partner, to the detriment of your own pleasure, leads to "self pilfering."

- In the marriage or the joint life, be generous, but do not make sacrifices. Men do not like victims. They love to care for weak and defenseless women while at the same time they want women to be strong. It is a paradox.

- If you still have a parental attitude towards your man, do not push it.

The man has no sexual urge for a "material" image. Do not be a doll! Be yourself!

And no tyranny! He needs to breathe!

People constantly make huge efforts to find the love of their life and to be loved and happy. Slogans inundate us from everywhere: "Love, be loved, or you will never be happy."

Love. How many crazy things are done for it. Everybody thinks that it is hard to find someone to love you and who reciprocates your feelings. But this is not true. It is much more complicated to keep the love of someone. If they were giving diplomas for this areas there would not be many excellent students because most people are good at putting off the people who they love the most.

When you are with a special person you always pretend to be someone that you are not. Love is not the most simple thing in the world, but we humans have the incredible talent to tangle it to maximum.

If one relationship goes normally, without unnecessary scandals and problems, people always begin to think that there is something rotten! That's because we are used to watching soap operas in which the main characters create problems themselves and that makes them more in love.

There are people who argue that true love lasts one hundred days; others, three years; and so on. Then the love boils and nothing and no one can return it. How long have most of your relationships lasted? Three months? Three years? Then they become an annoying and monotonous commitment, often ending with an ugly affair. And then you understand that the love, if it ever existed, is gone. Without warning, without time. When this happens most people fall into a deep depression. They start to blame themselves that they have made stupid mistakes and have missed the chance of their life. They feel sad that once again their heart has been broken. They cry for days, close themselves to the world and suffer unnecessarily. In the end, the result is swollen skin, over twenty kilograms gained, and a bunch of money spent on alcohol or psychiatrists.

And the love—is gone again!

There are people who put on their rose-colored glasses instead of investing money in tons of chocolate, going to the hairdresser, buying new clothes, and going out. They are impetuous to find a new love and they believe that this time they will keep this new love forever. And so they meet the next sap, the next betrayal, and the next new beginning. And embarking on a new beginning is the easiest thing. You do it at least three times a day. To keep the love of someone means to give up a part of yourself—to stop thinking about yourself and to start breathing for those who you love, because people choose the one who makes them feel special, the only one, unique, who makes every day looks different. But this requires much effort, not just a little makeup to erase the unpleasant pimple on your nose or saying "I love you" while watching your favorite soap opera.

Love is a selfish feeling—even when you think that you're ready to do anything for the one you love, the truth is that we are ready for anything to not be abandoned and to avoid suffering from lost love. Then we can pray, cry, and upset the world—but not to miss what we already had. Because let's not lie: love is a game, but nobody likes to lose! And to save someone's love is the greatest victory. To keep the love of a man is an art. And you should pay attention to it every day unless you want one morning to wake up holding a pillow instead of a man. Because to be alone, never having loved, is bearable but to have loved and to have let the love go away—this is a thought that would kill!

# *Stimulating the Relationship*

*L*ove is what can make you feel invincible. But love is also what can make you feel woeful without reason. Love has its advanced wonderful moments and these moments that can make you ask the question: "Am I in love?" It is very difficult to find the answer to this question. This question becomes heavy when the inertia of everyday life drags you down and when you become used to being with your boyfriend so much that you lose any stoppages, scruples, and concerns in the relationship. There is no more excitement but that peace which, together with the routine of the everyday life, leads to reflection of the value of your relationship in general.

How to revive the relationship? How to feel again that beautiful feeling, the happiness that you are together, that you love and belong to each other?

The easiest way to reignite the love in your relationship is to take a few days together, just the two of you. Spending time together, even for a few days, is extremely beneficial to your relationship. You know each other so well that you have learned the habits and the shortcomings. In the time that you will spend together you will find and rediscover these sweet features of your characters, which few people have had the privilege to know.

Spending time together nonstop during these one or two days or more will give you a clear idea whether you can live with this person, whether there are mutual compromises between you and him, and whether the love will accompany your days. A few days together without additional commitments will make you close again. You will rediscover your romantic feelings and you will feel how much you hold to each other. Again and again you will ascertain the strengths of his feelings and that you are the love of his life. When you go back to your old lifestyle you will feel and realize how much you love him and want to be with him. He is your blessing and your life.

If you do not live together, and now you have spent an inseparable couple of days together, it will be hard for you to leave him alone even just for a day. Ensure that you set some time just for you and him at least once every few months, even if only to go somewhere for the weekend or a few hours if you cannot afford a long breakaway commitment. Sometimes the life cycle, the work problems, and the commitments engage you so much that you actually forget the human next to you. You have accepted him as part of your life and you take him for granted. And for the agenda you have more important issues that deserve your attention. At that time, you have not really thought about it, but the truth is that you go a little away from your favorite person. Certainly the life of almost everyone is expressed by commitments and issues, but you should not let them distance you from your man. You should not allow them to take all your freedom and your mind as the most important things in life.

Much more important are your relations with the man next to you and it is good to give each other a little happiness, despite all the problems you've set and the problems that press you. Do not wait and try. For more valuable are the relations with the person next to you. He is the one who will help you when you need it. He is the one who is always behind you to protect you. He is more valuable than any problems of whatever nature they may be. A good time spent together, a few days with your favorite person somewhere, and this will certainly reflect favorably for you in every way. Love must be maintained as the flame of a fire.

You should always take care of it. To realize both how valuable and genuine the love is, it should be constantly experienced. Do it always without hesitation and keep the flame burning.

The most fortunate are those who understand that love is changing over time and do not live through a critical change of its manifestations. Present each other at least one day a month just for you. Let this day be Saturday. For the rest of the days of the week the enemies of romance and love—the daily routine, the stress, and the problems—will interfere with you spending quality time together. Twenty-four hours a day only concentrated on love—do you realize how difficult it is to achieve this? But the feeling is amazing! And forget phones, television, and children (leave them to your parents)!

**The day begins with a cup of coffee.** Today you should turn from Cinderella into a super-hot woman. To do this you must prepare all the details one day earlier: from clothes to the special products for the "erotic" breakfast that you will serve to your favorite man in the bed. He, of course, still has not woken up. You have available ten to fifteen minutes to take a quick shower and spread cream all over your whole body. When he opens his eyes he should see you enticing him, flying in a sexy satin dressing gown and leaving behind clouds of deliciously flavored cream, supplemented by aromatic coffee.

**Music and aroma.** For musical background, preferably use a disk of melodies that he loves. Entice him to bathe together, which means additional pleasures. Share the shower gel and...the naked bodies. For lunch, offer him a breathtaking perfume, an attractive appearance, tender skin, a caress on a suitable place, and the pleasant flavor of your lips.

At noon forget about the pan and the fatty dishes. A light salad, exotic sandwiches, aperitif, which he loves to drink at the bar with friends–well, today it provides an opportunity to drink with you privately. The goal is not to overeat but to eat something different, which is prepared quickly. It is strictly prohibited to watch TV! It harms the indigestion and the sterling love life. And sex on a full stomach is not right. You can talk, laugh, listen to music, and share "special" glances... Now it is time to make him help you for the light lunch. You prepared the breakfast alone. Find ways to make the preparing of the lunch a friendly game for both of you.

**Film for two.** If the love of a man goes through the stomach, then the love of a woman goes through the ears and the eyes. I already said that TV should be excluded during the day, but DVDs are a different story. Now is the time to watch an almost-love movie. "Almost" because if love is all, you risk your beloved falling asleep. Therefore you should choose a love story, mingled with little action or thriller. The afternoon "cinema" is a wonderful occasion to relax body to body, to share impressions and emotions, and even to talk about anything not related directly to the banal reality.

**Afternoon sleep or...** Yes, exactly as you read it: the kitchen is not just boring housewife territory, and could be a place for entertainment between the two. Do not think immediately of an erotic scene (on the table). Here's something easy: offer to prepare him an aphrodisiacal dinner (pate, asparagus, oysters, tomatoes, etc.) with white tablecloth, flowers, and candles on the table, and romantic music in the background. The talk on the table should be breathtaking (especially if you have not had sex that afternoon). But be careful with the alcohol; a few cups of wine relax, but more than a few will make you want to sleep.

**Under the light of candles.** You passed a day without television, turned off phones and have been completely isolated from the outside world. You are in front of a beautifully arranged special dinner table. Surely now is the time to talk about your relationship and feelings for each other. But in no case raise questions about financial problems in the family or problems at work. You need to talk about yourselves and what you feel for each other. This may be the magic beginning to restore an exciting relationship. But watch how you express yourself. The theme "feelings" is very delicate. This is also the best time for the exchange of "psychological" neckings.

Reward your man with special care, fork in his soul, and then pull it out with your feminine hand. And do not forget to tell him that today you were very happy. You can keep telling him the same thing later—in bed...

You do not want to separate rapidly from the initial passion, right? Well, then see the three major components of the fuel for male desire:

- **Mystery.** Men are hunters by nature. The less they know, the more they want to know. Do not rush into long explanations; instead, reveal a little less about your character.
- **Expectation.** As I already said, you should make him think about you all day. A playful text messasge will make him happy and you will be definitely inside his head.
- **Space.** Men dream of what is outside their range. If you are not constantly available and you have your own life, you will make him miss you and he will want you even more. Also, if after your first date he waited a week to call you, do not ask him why he took so long. Let him think that you have not been waiting for him to call; instead, allow him to think that you have been busy having fun and enjoying your life. By doing this you will show him that you are living a happy life and that you don't feel lonely or depressed. Let him know that he is just a pleasant addition to your happy life. This will show him that he does not have a 100-percent hold on you. He will become a little bit insecure and will do anything to win you.

On the other hand, if he is sure that he has a complete hold on you, he will become less interested and will start to play you as a toy. Do not allow this happen. Show that you are an independent woman who can be happy and content without by all means having a man. If you keep this simple rule he will be yours forever.

# Change Him with Patience

*I*f you want to change a man, do not rush with shock therapy. Pull his soul with cotton. To change a man is harder than climbing Mount Everest and more complex than repairing a car.

Yet some women manage to do it. Of course, there is no general recipe, but one rule always stays in force: Never apply shock therapy! Changing a man happens slowly—with patience, tenderness, and tact. To achieve success, never tell him:

"You do not take along with your friends. Are you ashamed of me?"
"I feel that you do not love my parents."
"You were so considerate to me in the beginning..."
"Do you think that I do not notice how you flirt with her?"
"You are like all men—sick and selfish."
"Wake up at last, should I always do everything?"
"You are all you life holding onto your mother's skirt."
"You are snoring again…"
"If you really loved me..."
"All my girlfriends are happy with their men…"
"God, how could I have married just you?"

Sociologists have specified that half of all women are trying to change their husbands. This case is not about domestic problems, but also about adjusting the vital road of the man. And this task is strictly classified. So if the man feels the impact of his wife, his reaction will be always very strong because he is the head of the family. Furthermore, there is no man who would want to be thought of as a little boy who needs education. Many women approach their activities very carefully and know that the groan and a variety of orders like: "You must do this" or "If you do not do that, then I..." are absolutely prohibited.

Here are some necessary diplomatic moves: Try to attract the curiosity of the man. This is the most important condition for success. The ideal place to implement the plans is in your bedroom. During sex man is allowed to be seduced. Here he is conciliatory and balanced. The sex, the ambition, and the self-confidence—these are the weaknesses of men, which women must remember.

Every woman has great imagination, intuition, and sensitivity. Exactly because of this, the creation of "your partner" is a real female hobby. Psychologists explain this with the eternal maternal instinct. Remember that planning the changes in your partner should also match his character, image, and desires.

Here are some tips to help change him:

- **His clothing.** "Do not ask why I have not bought you a new magnificent sweater." His statement that he does not want anything new should be disregarded.
- **Holiday and expenses.** In a thoughtful look and appropriate voice, say: "You need sun! These rains will destroy you." It is implied that the same also holds true for you.
- **His demeanor at the table.** Saying, "You know, my friend Mary yesterday complained that her husband constantly smacks while he eats," also means: "Eat quietly, honey!"
- **Jealousy.** Make your husband jealous by flirting with other men at his friend's birthday. Later at home, tell him: "I liked it tonight, I rested so well." Next time he will not even think about being away from you and he will never go again to that terrible leggy blonde.
- **Career.** Praise him more often. Say: "I am very proud of you. You have accomplished so much." Then you will see him putting in more effort to advance at work.

# *The Secrets of Eternal Love*

"They lived long and happily!" Is that really possible? Doesn't the love go away in time? Yet there are people who love each other after twenty years of coexistence. Maybe there is some secret to a healthy, happy relationship?

How do you maintain the eternal love amid the pot-bellies, the heavy snoring, and everything that the tales never tell us? Perhaps there is a recipe? Of course! It is simple and yet very complex to implement. It is different for every woman. You alone must find its true ingredients. Here are a few tested components:

- a well-groomed appearance
- five pegs—tact
- fashion magazines
- a dose of patience
- several minutes of silence

Early in the morning, allow several minutes of silence for him to calmly read the newspaper and drink his coffee. Do not forget to put in his bag a carefully prepared sandwich for lunch. When he tells you that he has an appointment and he will have lunch in a restaurant, do not call him shortly after the meeting under the pretext that you want to know how it went. Do not ask him questions even if you are dying to know with whom he had lunch. Go to coffee with his mother and befriend her. Men like it when their girlfriends get on well with their mothers. This makes them happy and they are satisfied that they have found the right woman for them. Do not forget to take his pants from the dryer, but do not mention, underline, or reproach that you did it. If he is nervous, act tactfully and do not make him do anything until he calms down.

Do not call him every two minutes after he gets off work to ask him: "Are you coming home?" This is a terribly unpleasant question! On the third time, he definitely will want to answer: "No, honey, I will be late!" Let him breathe free! He must go back home to you with his own desire!

Offer him a variety of dishes. Remember the Chinese proverb that the love of a man passes through his stomach.

Arm yourself with a dose of patience and spend all night with him in front of the TV while he watches sports programs. Do not mumble and do not show him that you are bored; instead, ask questions trying to show partiality to what he explains to you and do not start other topics.

To add a slight spicy taste to the relationship, check out a fashion magazine and choose the most tempting underwear! Wait for the weekend and spend two unforgettable days in bed! Sleep naked at night. The touch of your naked body will deliver pleasant feelings. Men like women to be naked because they like the female form. Therefore, go naked to the bathroom when you get up from bed. He finds you sexy and with your nakedness you will confirm this. Do not worry that you have gained some weight. He can tell you this but he will report it as a fact and will continue to enjoy your form.

As I already said earlier, never walk around at home with an uncomely appearance. He must see you always the way you looked when he first met you. He will assess your efforts. Do not stand in his presence with a facial mask and cucumber on your eyes! Learn to control your jealousy and do not step on the foot of the girl who smiles at him while you are dancing. Instead, surprise him as you wake him up at night—to make you warm in his arms.

Congratulations! Now you are a TOTAL Man Magnet who can make every man fall in love with you instantly!